HISTORY IN THE NATIONAL
                CURRICULUM.

375 : 9

Bedford Way Series
Published by Kogan Page in association with the Institute of Education, University of London

THE BEDFORD WAY SERIES

HISTORY IN THE NATIONAL CURRICULUM

Edited by
RICHARD ALDRICH

Contributors:
Richard Aldrich, John Slater, Peter Lee,
Alaric Dickinson, Dennis Dean

Published in association with
The Institute of Education, University of London

First published in 1991

Apart from any fair dealing for the purposes of research or private study, or criticism
or review, as permitted under the Copyright, Designs and Patents Act, 1988, this
publication may only be reproduced, stored or transmitted, in any form or by any
means, with the prior permission in writing of the publishers, or in the case of
reprographic reproduction in accordance with the terms of licences issued by the
Copyright Licensing Agency. Enquiries concerning reproduction outside those terms
should be sent to the publishers at the undermentioned address:

Kogan Page Limited
120 Pentonville Road
London N1 9JN

© Institute of Education, 1991

British Library Cataloguing in Publication Data

A CIP record for this book is available from the British Library.

ISBN 0 7494 0094 3

Typeset by DP Photosetting, Aylesbury, Bucks
Printed and bound in Great Britain by
Biddles Ltd, Guildford

Contents

Notes on Contributors

Richard Aldrich is Senior Lecturer in History of Education. His first degree was from Cambridge, his two research degrees from London. He has taught history in school and college of education and lectured at universities overseas, most recently in Canada and Brazil. He is president of the UK History of Education Society, past president of the Institute's Senior Common Room, and currently chairs its Academic Board. Publications include: *Sir John Pakington and National Education* (1979); *An Introduction to the History of Education* (1982); *Education: Time for a New Act?* (1985) with Patricia Leighton; *Dictionary of British Educationists* (1989) with Peter Gordon, and some 40 book chapters and journal articles.

Dennis Dean is Lecturer in History of Education. He has taught history in school and polytechnic and is an Honorary Fellow of the Polytechnic of North London. He has published in the *Journal of Contemporary History*, *Journal of Educational Administration and History* and contributed to A O'Day (ed.) *The Edwardian Age* (1979). Recent publications include: 'Planning for a postwar generation: Ellen Wilkinson and George Tomlinson at the Ministry of Education, 1945–51', *History of Education*, 15(2), 1986; 'Coping with colonial immigration, the Cold War and colonial policy. The Labour Government and black communities in Great Britain, 1945–51', *Immigrants and Minorities*, 6(3), 1987.

Alaric Dickinson is Senior Lecturer in Education with special reference to the teaching of history. He currently chairs the History and Humanities Department, and is a member of the Council and Education Committee of the Historical Association, and co-director of Project HIT (History and Information Technology). He has extensive

viii *History in the National Curriculum*

examining experience at 16+ and 18+. Current research interests
include new technology, and the development and assessment of
children's thinking in history. Publications include: *History Teaching
and Historical Understanding* (1978) (ed.) with P J Lee; *Learning History*
(1984) (ed.) with P J Lee and P J Rogers; *New History and New
Technology: present into future* (1986) (ed.) with F Blow.

Peter Lee is Senior Lecturer in Education with special reference to the
teaching of history. He is co-director (with Denis Shemilt) of the
Cambridge History Project which was set up in 1985 to work with
teachers to construct new 'A' level and 'AS' courses. Other current
interests include research into children's understanding of certain
historical concepts, and the analytical philosophy of history and its
implications for the teaching of history. Publications include: 'History
at the universities, the consumer's view: 1, Oxford history', *History*, 55,
1970; *History Teaching and Historical Understanding* (1978) (ed.) with A
K Dickinson; 'History teaching and philosophy of history', *History and
Theory*, 22, 1983; *Learning History* (1984) (ed.) with A K Dickinson and
P J Rogers; 'Children's concepts of empathy and understanding', with
R Ashby, in C Portal (ed.) *The History Curriculum for Teachers* (1987).

John Slater was HM Staff Inspector for History from 1974 to 1987. He
was principally responsible for *History in the Primary and Secondary
Years* (1985). From 1988 to 1990 he was Visiting Professor at the
London Institute. His inaugural lecture given in November 1988 was
published as *The Politics of History Teaching, a Humanity Dehuman-
ized?* (1989). He remains associated with the Institute as tutor and
organizer of inservice training in history.

Abbreviations Used

AT   Attainment Targets (with numbers, AT2 AT3)
CHP   Cambridge History Project
CSE   Certificate of Secondary Education
DES   Department of Education and Science
ERA   Education Reform Act of 1988
ETHOS   Enquiry into Teaching of History to the Over Sixteens
GCSE   General Certificate of Secondary Education
HCA   History Curriculum Association
HMI   Her Majesty's Inspectorate
HSU   History Study Unit
INSET   In-service Education of Teachers
KS   Key Stage (with numbers, KS1 KS2)
LEA   Local Education Authority
LMS   Local Management of Schools
NCC   National Curriculum Council
PC   Profile Component
PESC   Political; Economic, Technological and Scientific;
            Social and Religious; Cultural and Aesthetic
SAT   Standard Assessment Task
SCHP/SHP   Schools Council History Project (1972)/
            Schools History Project (1983)
SDU   School Designed Unit
SEAC   School Examinations and Assessment Council
TGAT   Task Group on Assessment and Testing

Preface and Acknowledgements

Since January 1989 when the National Curriculum History Working Group was set up and the writing of this book begun, there have been two Prime Ministers and three Secretaries of State for Education. At present these posts are occupied by John Major and Kenneth Clarke.

This book, though concerned with the immediate issues and uncertainties which surround the introduction of history into the National Curriculum and which have been exacerbated by these changes in political personnel, seeks essentially to reflect something of the experience and expertise of those who have dedicated their professional lives to the study and teaching of history.

The contributors to this volume would like to record their gratitude to all who helped at the several stages of writing and production: teachers and others who attended the three one-day conferences on 'History in the National Curriculum' at the Institute of Education, colleagues at the Institute and at Kogan Page. Our particular thanks are offered to Peter Keelan, Patricia Thomas and Deborah Hines.

Richard Aldrich
December 1990

Chapter One
Introduction

Richard Aldrich

The context

The Education Reform Act of 1988 is the most wide-ranging and revolutionary piece of educational legislation in English history. Enormous changes have been set in motion. It will take many years both to implement these changes (if indeed they are all to be implemented) and for their full effects to become known. In respect of curriculum, the Act empowers the Secretaries of State to specify programmes of study and attainment targets. Before making draft Orders, however, in England, the Secretary of State for Education and Science is required to make proposals to the National Curriculum Council(NCC), which in turn is required to consult and then make a report to the Secretary of State summarizing the views expressed on his proposals and the NCC's advice and recommendations. This volume is offered as a contribution to the process of consultation on and the construction of a history syllabus and assessment procedures for pupils aged five to 16.

In August 1990, at the time of writing, when the Secretary of State's response to the Final Report of the History Working Group has just been published, the overall pattern of educational change is still far from clear. A future government of a different political hue may well reverse some elements of change – for example those which relate to grant-maintained schools and the local management of schools. Indeed even the present Conservative government has now indicated its concern at some of the measures and procedures which it has itself introduced. For example, a retreat has been signalled over the testing of primary-age children in foundation subjects, while the possibility that some children may cease to study art, music and physical education at age 14 has been raised by the Secretary of State. In respect of history, the

Prime Minister herself has expressed alarm at the membership and Final Report of the Working Group.

Such a response indicates, only too clearly, the possible dangers of precipitate intervention by politicians in curriculum matters. It is a matter of record that Kenneth Baker, the former Secretary of State for Education and Science, and current chairman of the Conservative party, personally determined the composition of the History Working Group. He decided that it should include only one primary and one secondary schoolteacher. As to its agenda, his successor John MacGregor, in a letter of 10 August 1989 to its chairman Michael Saunders Watson, formally instructed the Group 'to prepare detailed programmes of study for all the history study units, spelling out the additional or more advanced content of knowledge – including dates, events, and people – that must be taught to pupils working towards each successive level of attainment'.

The Report

The Working Group followed this brief. As a result the Final Report was not written primarily with schools, teachers or children in mind. It was produced at the behest of, and for, the Secretary of State by a group which, at its conclusion, contained only one practising schoolteacher. It says little about the delivery of the curriculum or about styles of teaching. It is indeed, as the Prime Minister has correctly observed, a highly detailed document in which annexes and appendices predominate over text. Of the 205 pages in the Final Report some 14 pages are devoted to final appendices while another 14 are left blank. Although the Report is divided into no fewer than 11 chapters, Annex A to Chapter 6, which sets out programmes of study for each History Study Unit, occupies pages 33–113, while Annexes A and B to Chapter 7, which provide statements of attainment for each attainment target, take up pages 119–165.

Margaret Thatcher's concerns, as reported in *The Sunday Telegraph* of 15 April 1990, indicate that whereas in the 1980s some politicians (including Kenneth Baker) exhibited considerable confidence that they could reform education as a whole, and in particular improve the quality of history teaching in schools, doubts have now crept in. Though the Prime Minister's uncertainties in respect of history in the national curriculum are considered again later in this volume they are recorded here in detail for two reasons. First, they reflect the current confusions in the political mind which surround the place of history in the national curriculum; second, because in calling for 'great consultation and consideration' they provide a rationale for this book.

History was always going to be a difficult one because at the beginning we were not decided whether to put things like history and geography in a core curriculum or not, or in such a detailed foundation course. It is obvious that you must have some history and some geography: you are not a complete person unless you have that general knowledge. You simply must know, roughly chronologically, how things happened, what their significance was and why.

. . . Now the History Report has come out. It is very detailed. There were not many secondary school teachers on the syllabus-forming committee. I think it really must be put out to great consultation and consideration. My worry is whether we should put out such a detailed one. You see, once you put out an approved curriculum, if you have got it wrong, the situation is worse afterwards than it was before. At any given time a large number of teachers are teaching a subject extremely well. But if you take them off what they know has worked for years, far better than anyone else's syllabus, then you wonder: were you doing it right?

. . . History is not an extra subject, obviously. It is a vital subject and at least half of it should be British history. You can make it so exciting. But you cannot make it terribly exciting if a teacher is given no scope for using her creativeness. So that is really my concern.

Politics and education do not mix easily and well. Schools are particularly and properly concerned with education. Though it would be naive to suppose that they have no connections with the worlds of politics, economics and society, it would be equally naive to suppose that there are easy educational solutions to the problems of these wider worlds. It is true that some of the United Kingdom's economic competitors, for example France and Japan, have strongly centralized school systems and curricula, but other economically successful countries, such as the Netherlands, West Germany and the United States, do not. Just as there are no easy educational solutions to economic and political problems, so there are no easy political solutions to educational issues. For example, though there may be genuine concerns about the ways in which, in a free society, some teachers present history to their pupils, there are considerable dangers in central government control of history syllabuses, as the cancellation in 1988 and 1989 of school history examinations in the USSR because of the need to rewrite the history of the Stalin and Brezhnev eras showed.

A true National Curriculum – a democratic entitlement for all children to a core of knowledge, understanding and skills, appropriate both to themselves as individuals and to the society in which they live – is a worthy goal indeed. Such a goal, however, cannot be achieved simply by designating a list of ten subjects and four ages for national assessment, nor even by the production of separate reports on the curriculum and assessment of each subject. Attention must also be paid to such matters as staffing, buildings and materials. Sustained curriculum development also depends upon the involvement of teachers in the design, testing and evaluation of curriculum change. Margaret Thatcher's response to the Final Report of the History Working Group acknowledged the importance of such teacher professionalism, and signalled a reaction against the possible sterile aspects of an over-prescriptive centrally-imposed curriculum. Though such a response was in many ways encouraging, the government's rejection of certain aspects of the Final Report and amendment of others has increased the uncertainties surrounding the position of history, which is currently scheduled to be introduced into the National Curriculum from September 1991. John MacGregor's proposals have been sent to the National Curriculum Council which has been asked to report back by December 1990. They will then be sent to the School Examinations and Assessment Council for further advice on the Orders specifying assessment arrangements for history. The timetable is extremely tight.

The chapters
Given such uncertainties the authors of this volume do not pretend to provide permanent solutions to all the issues which currently surround the place of history in the National Curriculum. They do, however, seek to make two particular contributions to the debate. The first is to supply a detailed analysis of the Final Report of the History Working Group for England. Regrettably, though some references are made to the Welsh Report, it has not been possible to include a detailed considera-tion of that Final Report.

The chapter by John Slater examines the context of the Report, including its Interim predecessor, and the subsequent proposals of the Secretary of State. His analysis of the Final Report itself draws attention to its assumptions and philosophy, its concepts and meta-phors. Though welcoming much of the Report Slater identifies a number of weaknesses, for example: the absence of criteria for the selection of content; the defective and deficit view of children; the failure to distinguish adequately between objective truth and objective procedures; the problems of 'essential' and 'exemplary' information; the lack of attention paid to the need for resources and in-service training for teachers.

The second aim of this book is to examine three issues in respect of history in the school curriculum in a more fundamental way. These are: historical knowledge; assessment; and the historical perspective. Such an examination may be justified on two counts.

The first is that (as Margaret Thatcher's doubts reveal) whatever benefits recent political intervention in curricular matters may have produced, it has also led to confusions and controversies. In the last two years there has been more argument about history than about any other subject in the school curriculum. Unfortunately much of this argument has been based upon assertions and accusations, often by those who have minimal or no experience of teaching history in schools, but who have particular axes to grind. Heavily politicized debates about history in schools, as represented in some pamphlets and sections of the media, have obscured rather than clarified many of the key issues, and have provoked confrontation rather than resolution in respect of others. There is an urgent need for a fundamental professional analysis, one based upon knowledge and judgement. By this means the quality of the debate may be improved, so that the history curriculum of the 1990s may be reviewed and revised in accordance with fundamental historical and educational criteria.

A second justification for such an approach is connected with the subject of history itself. The teaching of history cannot stand still. Review and revision are essential. The history curriculum as set down for 1991 is itself an historical product. It proceeds from a whole range of immediate political, social, economic and educational factors and priorities. Both in its Interim and Final Reports the Working Group acknowledged this fact that, 'of all the subjects in the National Curriculum, history should not be prescribed in perpetuity but should be subject to periodic review'.

Thus the other contributions, by Peter Lee, Alaric Dickinson, and Richard Aldrich and Dennis Dean, while making reference to the reports of the History Working Group, bring more fundamental perspectives to bear on the topic of history in the National Curriculum.

In 'Historical Knowledge and the National Curriculum', Peter Lee examines what is meant by historical knowledge, and argues that real historical knowledge requires that children have both a workable framework of the past and some understanding of the discipline of history itself. In this analysis Lee draws on some of his own research into the processes of how children learn history, and stresses the need for further work in this area.

Alaric Dickinson begins his chapter by outlining the general assessment arrangements stipulated under the 1988 Act. He then turns to assessment in history and its implementation in the classroom, and provides a useful list of ten suggestions for good practice. He emphasizes that in the coming years the quality of assessment arrangements will be crucial in determining whether standards of teaching and learning in history are really improving, or whether they result in the narrowing of the subject and the imposition of excessive pressure on pupils and teachers.

The final chapter, by Richard Aldrich and Dennis Dean, brings the historical discipline to bear upon the teaching of history itself. They trace the nature and place of the subject in schools since the middle years of the nineteenth century, and show that the Education Reform Act is but the latest in a long line of curricular interventions by central governments. Their conclusion, however, which may be taken as a more general conclusion for the whole book, is that any central government intervention which neglects professional experience and wisdom has the potential not only to damage the quality of history in schools but also the quality of democracy itself.

In providing their analysis these members of the History side of the Institute's History and Humanities Department, all graduate historians and trained teachers themselves, have drawn upon several areas of expertise. The first is practical experience of the classroom. All of the contributors have taught history in schools. All have first-hand knowledge of how history has been, and is currently being, taught and studied in a range of schools. The second is their professional responsibility for training history teachers, both at initial and in-service levels. The third relates to their participation in historical associations and societies, in curriculum development in history, and in service on history examining boards. A fourth area of special expertise is provided by John Slater who, since his retirement from the post of Staff Inspector for History, has been an active and valued part-time member of the department. Finally it should be noted that the contributors have had the privilege of learning from, and contributing to, a long departmental tradition of thought, discussion, teaching and publication about the place of history in the school curriculum. This process has a very long history in itself, and pre-dates both the recent reforms and the professional careers of the authors themselves.

Chapter Two
History in the National Curriculum: the Final Report of the History Working Group

John Slater

Antecedents and birth

Does the Final Report of the History Working Group demonstrate more continuity than change, more similarities with its forebears than differences? Does it remind us that recent thinking on a national history curriculum has, in the words of the Report 'zig-zagged or regressed'? For some years much educational thinking has created a benevolent climate for the advice of the Working Group. David Eccles opening the secret garden of the curriculum in 1970, James Callaghan's speech in 1976 at Ruskin College, Oxford, Shirley Williams with her Green Paper and debating the Great Debate in 1977, all served to remind us that the absence of government influence on the curriculum was more the result of an unquestioned tradition than any statutory limitation. Since 1977 much writing and even more talk from the centre, particularly from HMI, have provided not only a favourable climate for the Report, but forebears with detectable family likenesses. In 1977 Her Majesty's Inspectorate (HMI) published *Curriculum 11 to 16* which saw the curriculum as eight areas of experience. One paper looked particularly at the role of history. It emphasized skills, particularly those associated with the evaluation of evidence and with attempts to enter into a degree of understanding of the predicaments and points of view of other people. The content was not defined but the paper said that skills should develop progressively within a broad, balanced framework of British, world and local history. In 1980 the importance of history was given some emphasis in another HMI publication, *A View of the Curriculum*. In 1984 Keith Joseph, the Secretary of State, devoted a whole speech to a considered defence of history, which received wide support. He supported the development of skills, stressed understanding (he had already posed to HMI the question as to what the learning of history did to develop the reasoning of young people as opposed to their memories) and emphasized the importance of a framework of knowledge of the past, particularly that of Britain, for a nation which he saw clearly as a pluralist, multicultural society.

In 1985 HMI published *History in the Primary and Secondary Years*. As Keith Joseph had done, it offered a rationale of history in the curriculum, not only in terms of the needs of society at large but also of the individual development, interests and enthusiasms of pupils. It detailed historical skills and offered a taxonomy for their progressive acquisition and assessment. It defined content only in very general terms and repeated the need for a balance between British, world and local history. However, it did offer a list of some 50 first- and second-order concepts to which pupils should have been introduced by the time they left school at the age of 16. Many of these were period- or topic-specific. It also argued that history has an important role to play in reducing misunderstandings and ignorance about the contemporary world and suggested a number of themes in contemporary society of sufficient importance to justify being put into their historical context. *History in the Primary and Secondary Years* recognized that its criteria for selecting content could produce a considerable diversity of content within the English school system, and argued for a minimum basis of shared knowledge as a common framework or map of the past. This proposal owed much to the speech of Keith Joseph and it anticipated some aspects of current thinking about a National Curriculum for history.

History in the Primary and Secondary Years also considered issues such as women and history, history in a multicultural society and the problems of bias, prejudice and indoctrination. It devoted a whole chapter to necessary resources. In sum, it offered a starting point for teachers to develop their own schemes of work and relate content to skills, and it suggested appropriate teaching methods and available resources, and also means of assessing pupil and teacher progress. Above all it proposed an agenda of shared criteria for the *selection* of content.

In 1988 *Curriculum Matters 5 to 16: History* was published. It embodied and developed many of the ideas discussed in *History in the Primary and Secondary Years*. But there were significant differences. In particular it offered detailed suggestions on the factual content of a history syllabus, although the criteria for selection were unclear. It appeared uncritically to accept history as a socializing subject, transmitting the culture and shared values of society. However, this issue had not been identified, let alone discussed, in previous HMI writing. It could be argued that this view was at variance with the closing section of the earlier document which stated:

> Thinking historically strengthens our knowledge of our memories and gives us procedures to evaluate and learn from them. These procedures may increase our knowledge and belief in certain shared values. Equally they may instil a sense of informed unease about ourselves and the societies in which we live. But without the evidence and an historical context our attitudes may cling to stereotypes and seek refuge in unreal aspirations.

The birth of the Final Report, together with its slightly older and awkward sibling called Interim Report, was the result not only of the hard work and dedication of the midwives sitting on the Working Group but also of the varieties of advice that was variously sought, gratuitously offered or imposed. What all this advice had in common was a belief in the importance of history and the influence it could have on children. The most immediate factors affecting the work of the Group were its terms of reference, together with the supplementary guidance given to its Chairman by the Secretary of State. They stated that the Group should 'leave scope for teachers to use their professional talents and skills to develop their own schemes of work, within a statutory framework which is known to all. It was the task of the Working Group on History to advise on that framework for history.' The use of the word 'framework', and references to the professional talents and skills of teachers would have been welcomed by the Group. So too would the emphasis on the differing abilities and maturities of pupils, and the particular issue of the most able pupils and those with special educational needs; on the importance of the relevance of a national curriculum to, and links with, 'pupils' own experience and background and their practical application . . .'; on the importance of equal opportunities for boys and girls; and on the requirement that the Group's work should take account of the ethnic diversity of the school population and society at large.

The requirement that the core of programmes of study should be 'British history, the record of its past' was unlikely to be seriously controversial. More controversial was the emphasis given to the political, constitutional and cultural heritage of British history and the omission of any mention of economic, technological and social heritages. Some may have been uneasy that programmes of study should help pupils 'come to understand how a free and democratic society has developed', but the Secretary of State's words were couched in general terms and could be variously and flexibly interpreted.

Few teachers would have felt threatened by the requirement that the Working Group's advice should foster 'a sense of place and time and a grasp of chronology and historical techniques; and the capacity for historical understanding based on sound evidence. They [the programmes] should assist the progressive acquisition of skills in the collection, objective analysis, interpretation, discriminating use and reporting of evidence from a variety of sources.' They would not have resisted some emphasis on the importance of good written English and numeracy. And who could have questioned the importance attached by the Secretary of State to history as 'interesting, exciting and enjoyable'?

Not all were convinced by the report of the Task Group on Assessment and Testing (TGAT) published in 1988 which included recommendations for the work of subject groups, which was embodied in the government's statement to Parliament in June 1988. It was not clear at the time, nor could it have been because there was little evidence to support clarity, as to whether TGAT's recommendations applied equally across the curriculum and in particular to history. However, all that the History Working Group was required to do was to 'take account' of the government's 1988 response and to 'offer advice in broad terms about assessment and testing'. There was no requirement for the Working Group to accept the TGAT recommendations if they felt them to be invalid, unworkable or irrelevant.

The profession and other interested parties were, I suspect, cautiously reassured by the terms of reference given to the History Working Group. There may have been some lingering doubts for example concerning the supplementary guidance to the Chairman that 'the programmes of study should provide a detailed description of the content, skills and processes which all pupils need to be taught'. Did this suggest the framework might become a dense lattice-work which would leave less scope for teachers to use their professional talents than the terms of reference suggested? Why was there no reference to oracy? Most worrying was the virtual absence of any reference to the resources necessary to deliver the new curriculum. Time is a resource, but the reference made by the Secretary of State to its allocation, particularly for pupils aged 11 to 14, was more generous than most schools enjoyed, and may have said more about Mr Baker's belief in the importance of history than his knowledge of the realities of school timetables. Failure to require some consideration of the resource implications of the advice

of the Working Group seriously weakened the credibility of the
subsequent reports.

The authors of the Report
The Working Group who wrote this Final Report and its Interim
predecessor were appointed by the Secretary of State. There seems little
evidence to support the conspiratorial view that it was packed with
deferential, pliable place-men and women. However the absence of one
considerable national expert on assessment and on the development of
children's learning, after his serious consideration, not only weakened
the professional cutting edge of the Group but suggested the possibility
at least of factors at work not solely concerned with qualifications and
professional relevance.

There were, including the Chairman, ten full-time members of the
Group and two subsequent secondments. The Group demonstrated an
impressive commitment to the production of their Report and must
have worked desperately hard to meet ministerial deadlines. They
included a Director of Education, a Chairman of a County Council, a
Senior Adviser, two university historians and two teacher trainers.
There were two teachers, one each from the primary and secondary
sectors. Some other members of the Group had regular contact with
pupils in classes and others had impressive and recent teaching
experience. Three were women. All were white.

The Group was serviced and advised by an able team of civil servants
and the Staff Inspector for History, who was described as an 'observer'.
This term has been in use for some time within HMI to describe its
relationship with independent bodies. It suggests a passive, external
role, neither referee, adviser, nor arbitrator. In fact HMI can play a
crucial role in suggesting, drafting, warning, encouraging and influenc-
ing. However the independence of the Working Group would have
depended on its understanding of the nature and the limitations of HMI
role and so on their freedom to examine critically HMI advice and, if
they so chose, to reject it entirely. In the same way the ability of HMI
convincingly to monitor and critically evaluate a national history
curriculum in the future would also depend on a general understanding
of the distinction and gap between HMI advice and that given to the
Secretary of State by the Working Group. Of course there is no public
evidence on the Working Group's discussions. There is no reason to
suppose that the delicate distinction between the advice of HMI and the
civil servants and the ability of the Working Group to assert its
independence was not happily maintained.

The Final Report and its predecessor

This chapter concentrates on the Final Report but its Interim predecessor, and the reaction of the Secretary of State to it, cannot be ignored. There is no doubt that it is a stronger and much more persuasive document. It re-emphasizes British history without seriously compromising a European and world context and has offered a much sounder and more usable strategy for the teaching of what are now called History Study Units (HSUs). It has made attainment targets more rational by reducing them from five to four and argued strongly against separating the knowledge from its context and complementary skills by placing it in a distinct attainment target. It argues this case powerfully and persuasively. In particular it offers a clear warning on 'official history' if specified historical information is placed within a separate attainment target. The Group writes 'Many people express deep concern that school history will be used as propaganda; that governments of one particular hue or another will try to subvert it for the purposes of indoctrination or social engineering . . . We hope our recommended attainment targets may allay such fears.' This important statement would have been appreciated and, we suspect, endorsed by one of Mr MacGregor's predecessors, Keith Joseph. But Mr MacGregor's letter to the Chairman of the School Examinations and Assessment Council, written after the publication of the Final Report, suggests that he is not wholly persuaded. 'I attach great importance to knowledge . . . I look to the Council to consider and let me know whether assessment against the attainment targets, as recommended in the Report, will reliably reflect a pupil's level of knowledge within each study unit'. But the words of the Working Group on this issue are certainly not those of poodles whimpering, or of cringing deference.

The choice of History Study Units is more comprehensive and less eccentrically selective than in the Interim Report: the Second World War is now included and some of the themes less chronologically constrained than they were, for example, for the history of Russia. There are more opportunities to study the histories of parts of Asia and Africa and the Americas, and considerably more to study their peoples in terms of their own achievements and cultures before the impact of European settlement and colonizations. A School Designed Unit is now available in Key Stage 4 for pupils aged 14 to 16. The total number of History Study Units in Key Stages 2 to 4 has been reduced from 28 to 23. Furthermore the Final Report has begun the difficult task of identifying ten levels of achievement and relating them to the four attainment targets.

The Final Report: assumptions, philosophy and thrust
The changes between the Working Group's two Reports offer clear
evidence that its members, having sought the views of a wide range of
individuals and groups, listened to, considered and were influenced by
them. Evidence for the underlying philosophies and assumptions in the
Final Report are found mainly in Chapters 1 (History in the School
Curriculum), 2 (Structure of the History Course), 3 (The Essence of
History) and 4 (The General Rationale for our course of School
History), together with scattered references throughout the Report,
particularly in Chapter 10. This section will consider broad issues of
strategy. The following section will look more particularly at what
teachers will be expected to deliver, History Study Units, assessment,
and support for implementing the curriculum.

The Final Report provides a clear and well argued case for history in
schools which will not only be helpful to parents, employers and others,
but in the main be acceptable to teachers. The first four chapters could
well provide, if opportunities are allowed, a useful agenda item for
discussing the implementation and future development of a national
history curriculum. There is likely to be general acceptance of the
following points:

(a) the careful and well-argued stress on the interdependence of
historical skills and information and more particularly the Report's
considered rejection of an attainment target specifically concerned
with knowledge.

(b) its lucid, uncluttered statement on the purposes of school history,
more particularly: an understanding of the present by putting it in its
historical context; giving pupils a sense of identity including their
own 'cultural roots' and 'shared inheritances' (always a significant
plural); to help an understanding of other cultures and societies
which is rooted in toleration and a respect for cultural variety; to
train the mind by disciplined enquiry, systematic analysis, argument,
logical rigour and the search for truth related to the historians'
discipline of constructing accounts of the past by the rigorous testing
of evidence which is often incomplete; to enrich other areas of the
curriculum and to prepare pupils for adult life.

(c) the need for a national curriculum is evidence based, drawn from the
results of HMI surveys and reports.

(d) the Report recognizes the contribution of GCSE and the Schools
History Project to much of the new thinking about history, and
wisely avoids entering the recent public debate, well-intentioned but

often ill-informed, and unhelpfully polarizing the distinction between traditional and new forms of history.

(e) placing the case for a national history syllabus in the wider perspectives of the structure of the English and Welsh school systems and a mobile population. Pupils are entitled neither to be bored by repetitions nor unnecessarily disconcerted by gaps in content as they move from primary to secondary schools, or change schools as their families move around the country.

(f) finally, the Report summarizes its overall objectives in the following words 'To design a course of history for pupils from the age of 5 to age 16 which gives equal weight to knowledge, understanding and skills; a course which will combine rigour, intellectual excitement and planned programming.'

Well, so far, and in terms of a general strategy, so good.

Reservations, doubts and uncertainties
Despite the original terms of reference the scope for teachers to develop their professional talents remains limited. Just how limited will appear when we consider in greater detail the History Study Units. The Report has nothing to say on the processes of implementing, evaluating and evolving the history curriculum as a *partnership* between the centre and the profession. There remains a considerable imbalance between the influence of the centre and the autonomy and experience of the profession. For example, a discussion on the selection of HSUs and of themes within them is difficult if there are no publicly declared criteria for their selection. But the Report is largely silent on this issue. The centre knows best. References to 'the selection and design of HSUs reflects this variety' (of British culture and its historical origin) or 'essential elements of Welsh, Scottish and Irish history have been included' are more dismissive than informative. School Designed Units (SDUs) are where the initiative of enterprising and thoughtful teachers might be expected best to flourish. But they are granted only some 17 per cent of the total time for pupils aged between 7 to 16 years, and these units are strictly constrained in their design and frequently in their general subject matter. The Working Group does not seem to have great faith in the status of SDUs. In Key Stage 4, for example, non-examination pupils who may be obliged to follow a reduced course will not be allowed to study a School Designed Unit. It is the first easy casualty of compromise rather than an element in learning jealously to be guarded.

A second imbalance is detectable, that between teaching and

learning, between the teacher and the pupil as a resource. In the key paragraph on the purposes of school history in the Report's first chapter the last purpose is 'to prepare pupils for adult life'. This objective is, we suppose, related to that metaphor-cliché of educational talk, 'schools are a preparation for life'. It is an oddly pre-natal view of schools which diminishes, or in the case of the Report, seems totally to ignore, the variety of enthusiasms and hobbies to do with the past which can be found within any one classroom. They excite, often make considerable demands, and produce memorable experiences. They need no more justification than that. Nor does the Report recognize, not explicitly anyway, the research of people like John West, working with young children in what has become to be known as Key Stages 1 and 2 which estimated that the vast majority – perhaps as high as 80 per cent – of knowledge that young children had of the past came from outside the school. The perceptive teacher recognizes the pupil as a resource but the content and timing of pupils' knowledge and interests are unpredictable, not always best nurtured in tightly defined and unnegotiable syllabuses. In a phrase, used twice in the Report, and in itself revealing, the Group refers to 'the need to reveal to pupils that history is interesting, exciting and enjoyable.' How very patronizing and *de haut en bas*! Many teachers, particularly those of younger children, know of the enjoyment which already exists in their pupils and which they can sensitively encourage but not too bossily develop. Unfortunately, there are still some teachers, many schemes of work and, we dare say, some History Study Units, which are more likely to close windows and dampen enthusiasm than to be effective agents of revelation.

While the Report wisely reminds us of the need to be sensitive to the different levels of pupils' intellects and understanding, and of the particular needs of the most able and those with special educational needs, it is remarkably silent on the experience and background of pupils or of the ethnic diversity, not just as a characteristic of English society as a whole but as a feature which may vary between neighbouring schools in the same city or within schools – even within single classrooms.

Does the virtual silence of the Group on these issues contain some hidden messages and lurking assumptions? That education is synonymous with schooling? That what children learn about the past depends on what they are taught? And that teachers and members of the Working Group know, have experienced and understood more than pupils in schools?

There are pupils in schools who have experienced violence, racial intolerance, drug trafficking, other cultures and beliefs, life in other countries or sporting or artistic achievements, all outside the experience indeed possibly the comprehension of some of their teachers. The author well remembers having heard a young pupil playing magically on the violin being told by his headmaster that 'he is one of our less able pupils'. No doubt the experience and achievement that was central to that young boy's life was outside the experience and comprehension of his headteacher.

In the short section on 'History and Values' we read that 'teachers should not hold back from dealing with controversial questions on morality or values which unite or divide ... material should be introduced at a time when pupils have sufficient maturity to possess the critical faculties to handle it appropriately.' We find a clutch of concealed assumptions here. It is assumed that there *is* a generally recognized level of maturity characterized by an understood appropriateness, although for whom and for what is not stated. It also assumes that young people, whatever their experiences of life may have been, have insufficient maturity to cope with related moral issues and value judgements and that, presumably, the adult world in general, and teachers and educators in particular, constantly demonstrate their ability to do so. Well, not the author of this chapter for one! In fact, this short section contains a deal of muddled thinking, having much in common with those who seek always to separate knowledge from understanding, and contradicts the powerful and sensible arguments to the contrary deployed elsewhere in the Report. To make sense of it depends on the supposition that there are identifiable and generally understood terminal points in the development of pupils' understanding which enable one to say, 'Ah, now you have it – 8 out of 10 for maturity of judgement. Now we can start on value judgements and controversial issues!' I suspect it is an innocent and simplistic view of the world for most of us including pupils in schools, let alone those who have may have experienced, for example, family violence, racial attacks or the experience of growing up with a different religious belief from those generally held. History, unlike say, much of mathematics, craft technology, athletics or music, does not consist of identifiable targets as necessary destinations before further progress can take place. Historical thinking can never say 'Now I know enough. At last I have understood everything.' More modestly it progressively decreases our ignorance and seeks to reduce and clarify our misunderstandings. But the starting point is never a *tabula rasa*.

It is obviously of importance for the Report to stress the levels of children's historical understanding as helping define attainments and more particularly levels of attainment within them. Equally important is a recognition of the extent of children's knowledge and the diversity of their interests and enthusiasms. These can affect and enrich teaching styles, and should surely have influenced the selection and pattern of History Study Units and particularly the range of choice within them.

There are also some odd statements on values in the section on 'The Purposes of History' which need to be explained, amended or omitted. References to 'understanding shared values' and later to 'broadly shared values' need clarification, as does, more urgently the requirement that 'the study of history of other societies from their own perspectives' should be pursued, 'without devaluing British achievements, values and traditions.' All this looks too much like conclusions desperately searching for supportive evidence. Myths are to be challenged not perpetuated.

Concepts and metaphors

These last comments draw attention to another weakness in much of the writing of this Report. It is its choice of words, particularly its key concepts. Problems arise from the use of 'balance', 'breadth', 'coherence', 'objectivity', and to a lesser extent, 'relevant', 'appropriate' and 'sufficient'. What all these words have in common is that they are armtwisters. They demand acceptance. Who could possibly oppose them? Is anyone foolish enough to defend 'imbalance', 'narrowness', 'incoherence', 'subjectivity', 'irrelevance', 'inappropriateness' and 'insufficiency'? They are also words which have long been part of curricular writing from the DES and HMI. They are now a little shopworn. The objection to clichés is not that they are untrue but that their familiarity breeds an uncritical acceptance. If, in addition, some of the clichés are also metaphors, such as 'balance', 'breadth', 'coherence', then misunderstandings may be compounded, particularly if they in their turn are explained with yet more metaphors, for example, 'organic whole'. We also have unhelpful references elsewhere in the Report to a 'web of causation' and the 'spiral effect of cause and consequence', related we assume, to the visual metaphor of the helix. Now there is nothing wrong with using metaphors, provided they are recognized as such and that there is some shared perception among the readers of the Report of the realities which those metaphors seek to illuminate.

Let us look a little more closely at some of the words that are used. 'Breadth' is a spatial metaphor and, separated from its usual ally 'depth', it runs the danger of rapid journeys over clearly mapped territory allowing insufficient time for reflection, distraction or three star sites which, as Michelin would say, are 'worth the diversion'. As the term is used in the Report it describes a variety of content to guarantee (another spatial metaphor coming up) the various 'dimensions' in the study of history, for example, technological as well as political, ancient as well as modern, different cultures, a variety of inheritances and a wide range of skills. The Report also says that the broad content should 'support the complete range of attainment targets of history'. Attainment targets represent a valid strategy but they are artificial constructs imposed on history for a particular and partly non-historical purpose. Surely it is not the task to organize a history syllabus which supports attainment targets but to construct a history syllabus which is supported by those targets? Although this section provides a useful checklist for those planning a history syllabus the abstract-figurative concept of 'breadth' does not supply an historical rationale or a comprehensible criterion for the selection of content. A reference to 'breadth' is not in itself a justification for the inclusion of ancient as well as modern history.

Is 'balance' a helpful concept? If 'breadth' suggests 'area', 'balance' suggests equilibrium between contrasted but equally weighted elements. It has often been used in the past to justify a simplistic study of complex issues often reduced to two contrasting points of view, frequently at the expense of understanding either one of them thoroughly. It can urge the search for a kind of compatibility of worth which can inhibit commitment and threaten moral outrage. 'Well, next week, boys and girls, the case *for* genocide'. The Report sees 'balance' also in terms of content – curriculum planning as a form of compensation. The modern world is compensated (balanced) by the ancient, the rich by the poor, men by women. A balance of dimensions also justifies the History Study Units' PESC formula (political; economic, technological, scientific; social and religious; cultural and aesthetic). The balance needs distinct and separate items to weigh. Are the PESC categories examples of a metaphorical take-over, creating distinctions, separateness, and comparability where often they do not exist? Much will depend not only on how the PESC formula is defined in each Unit but also on how it is used.

A 'balance' of points of view was how the word was used in the Education Act No 2 1986 and to which the Report refers. But it is also implicit in the 'General Rationale for School History' section in the Report when, under the heading of 'balance', reference is made to preparing young people to be citizens (are people without the vote not citizens?), and their need 'to make up their minds with the knowledge and skills to do so'. About what? Between what? We assume between a 'balance' of opposing views. Once again a metaphor which could usefully have been used retrospectively to clarify concrete examples is apparently used prospectively as a spurious criterion for selection and planning.

And what about 'coherence'? A coherent course, says the Report, 'fits together into an organic whole with its component parts able to stand by themselves as well as supporting each other' (well at least it covers their options). In particular the HSUs must 'deliver' (another popular DES metaphor) 'the attainment targets and PESC, have explicit links within and across the Key Stages and supply a framework of chronology.' Much of this will be uncontroversial and once again the artificial constructs of attainment targets and PESC should be seen as servants rather than as masters of pupils' learning. But 'coherence' is too loose a term to be useful. This is not an argument for incoherence but merely to point out that there are varieties of coherence. The Schools History Project (SHP) was criticized for the incoherence of its content, and by some measuring rods it was. Nevertheless it represented one of the most considered and coherent history syllabuses that had been published. But the measuring rods were different, explicit, argued and concrete. There are also syllabuses, with much in common with proposals of the Report, the coherence of which relates to the location of the school in its region and to its available resources. A course may also be coherent to a group of pupils, or to individual pupils, because it relates to their war games, grandma's memories, the house or estate they live in, or to the visits they made during their holidays. Does coherence need to apply to everything? Is there no case for the random, the quirky and the unpredictable? As adults much of our reading, TV viewing, visits to museums and galleries and holidaying are bound together only by a love of the past and other cultures. Should the pattern and enjoyment of such experiences be exclusively adult?

Objectivity
The Report recognizes the imcompleteness of historical evidence, the variety of interpretations of the past, the value-judgements made in selecting, or omitting, content, the changing perspectives of the past resulting from the changing circumstances of the present, and the absolute need to base historical statements on available evidence. But where does the Report stand on 'historical truth' and 'objectivity'? On

balance I think we can understand their message, but given the bluff and widely held commonsense view that there is an objective view of the past waiting to be seized and communicated and an historical truth acceptable to all historians, it is a pity that the views of the Working Group on this important issue were not spelt out more clearly. We read early on that 'historians cannot therefore describe the past with the objectivity of natural scientists.' However six pages earlier we read of the 'search for the truth' and four pages later that 'pupils should come to understand that historical objectivity is an ideal always to be pursued, though it may never be completely realised', while Level 9 Attainment Target 2 asks pupils to 'discuss a range of problems and issues encountered when trying to make history objective.' Apart from the difficult and value-laden question as to whether it does more harm than good to pursue unachievable ideals 'may never' suggests 'just might'. Or does it? Unlike much of the Report which has some internal consistency these quotations suggest a committee too good-naturedly allowing contrasted points of view to fly their conflicting flags.

History in the Primary and Secondary Years explicitly discussed this issue and attempted to distinguish between objective content and objective procedures. 'The inevitable selection and rejection of content are value-judgements, and the content of history curricula can never be either objective or value free. However the *procedures* of history . . . are objective as they cannot be modified either by the ideas bing examined or by the conclusions we may hope to reach.' That distinction seems to be consistent with most of what the Report says. But ambiguities should have been eliminated and the distinction more explicitly discussed.

Official prose style also surfaces on occasions throughout the whole Report in its use of the words 'appropriate', 'relevant', 'sufficient', 'satisfactory'. They mean little unless they are qualified with a preposition and a phrase expressed in concrete terms. However there is a little more to it than just careless writing. At a time when the effective implementation, evaluation and evolution of a national curriculum depends on a good working partnership between the centre and the professionalism of teachers, it is simply not good enough to leave unclear just who defines what is 'relevant', 'appropriate' and 'sufficient', for whom and for what purposes.

History Study Units and attainment targets

What affects teachers and pupils most directly are the front line troops of the Report, the History Study Units and their related attainment targets. These are what have to be delivered. On them depends the

ability to challenge, interest and enthuse pupils; to give helpful support
to the inexperienced or uncertain teachers while at the same time
allowing the enterprise of those with exciting ideas to develop and
initiate change.

Do they, as the Working Group was asked to do, provide a balanced,
broad, coherent and common syllabus which allows scope for the
talents of teachers, is relevant to pupils' 'experience and background'
and takes 'the ethnic diversity of the school population and society at
large'? Are they selected and described with a comprehensible rationale
and related to a clear and workable strategy? Do they represent a
programme which can be resourced and taught?

The general but clear statements about a core of British, including
local, history in its mainland European and world context, together
with a mix of periods and places, and including study of other cultures
through their experiences, with the need for depth as well as longer
studies in development, offer a simple, initial and, in the main,
acceptable framework.

This in itself would be insufficient if we are to reduce the repetitions
and gaps in learning which frequently occur as pupils move from
primary to secondary or around the country. But this mobility is very
Anglo-centric. Do families not move eastwards and westwards across
Offa's Dyke? It is odd then, that the proposals of the Welsh History
Committee's recommendations are different from those in the Final
Report from England. Odd too that in *no other subject* in the National
Curriculum are different curricula proposed in England and Wales. Did
HMI and civil servants never talk to each other? 'Shared inheritances'
evidently do not include history curricula! The Report defines some
general criteria which explain the selection of some of its HSUs, for
example that they support the attainment targets, include separate
studies in depth and development, together with suggestions for their
teaching. But these criteria are *not* offered as a framework for teachers'
choice, but as a justification for the Report's prescription. What is
required by the Report is not, for example, *a* study in depth or *a* study
through time, but *our* study in depth or through time. Thus the Report
not only fails to implement some of the requirements of its terms of
reference but would not enable us to give a positive answer to the first
question posed at the beginning of this section.

However the Report proposes what many would feel to be a usable
and very helpful framework for planning and evaluating each Study
Unit. It is no bad thing for teachers to have to write a considered
rationale for the units of work they propose to teach, to consider some

of the particular issues, insights and ideas they seek to develop in those units, to indicate what aspects of a major theme they choose to emphasize and to list the key facts on which the developing skills and understanding of the pupils depend. And the PESC formula, potentially, acts as a constant reminder to teachers that in the planning and evaluating of units of work, events in the past must not be too narrowly based or appear to ignore the wide range of human achievement. This formula could well give valuable support to young and inexperienced teachers while leaving scope for those who wish to develop ideas of their own.

However, the Working Group could not resist the temptation to fill out the framework with lists of concepts, necessary knowledge, and themes all of which *have* to be taught. It is a sad case of well not being left alone. Thus concepts are listed in each unit which presumably have to be taught. It is perhaps a minor matter that many are not really concepts at all but are historical ideas or terms. More worrying is the relating of concepts to particular key stages. Are pupils below the age of 14 really not supposed to be aware of, for example, 'migration', 'propaganda', 'free-trade', 'patriotism'? There are also odd omissions: 'immigration', but not 'emigration'; no 'censorship' in the unit on Printing and Writing, or 'heresy' or 'schism' in the unit on Reformation and Religious Diversity in Western Europe in the Sixteenth Century, and have not 'monetarism' and 'market economy' earned a place in that on Britain in the Twentieth Century? It is assumed that all listed concepts have to be studied. Nothing is said to suggest they can be added to or considered at other key stages.

Essential and exemplary information

It is useful to offer, *as examples*, the kind of information needed to make sense of a particular theme. The Report's suggestions are under the headings of 'Essential and Exemplary Knowledge.' Like the concepts listed it is an odd mixed bag which the experienced teacher could cope with but which would puzzle many. The first heading includes some specific knowledge such as 'Declaration of Independence 4th of July 1776', 'The Invasion of Poland 1939', 'The Battle of Trafalgar 1805'. Some entries are far less specific and are general headings which contain knowledge but are not themselves knowledge, such as 'The Colonial Empire and Slavery', 'Tsarist Rule', 'Relations between England, Ireland, Scotland and Wales' (sic!) and others which are even more general and less helpful; 'Church and Parish', 'Unrest and Protest', 'Independent India'. Bewilderment is not decreased when we read that the information in the 'Essential' column 'must be taught.' It is not clear whether the 'Exemplary' information must be taught. 'Exemplary' is an ambiguous word and it is not clear whether the knowledge is required or merely a best-buy that is strongly recommended to the consumers for serious consideration. Needless to say, the knowledge in this column appears to be no less arbitrarily chosen and eccentrically mixed. One hears increasingly the clatter of bucks being passed from Elizabeth House to the National Curriculum Council in York.

But the arbitrary and often eccentric selection of content within the units is hardly surprising in the absence of declared criteria. One suspects that it is not that they have been withheld, but that they simply do not exist. Why, for example:

(a) in the unit on 'Life in Britain since 1930' are references to unemployment limited to the 1930s and not to any later periods?

(b) in 'Food and Farming through History' is the emphasis on 'grain production'? Many schools are in parts of the country where wealth depended on fish, or cattle, or fruit, or horticulture and allotments. Why, in spite of the title of this unit is nothing to be considered after the 18th century?

Similarly, why is a study of 'Land Transport through History' (another misleading title) cut off in 1850 before the Railway Age had its full impact on British society, and the arrival of the motor car?

(c) in one of the two studies on the built environment is the study of public buildings limited to castles and cathedrals? They are rich subjects in *some* parts of the country. But why not railway stations, or town halls, or cinemas and theatres, or schools?

(d) in the study of 'The British Empire at Its Zenith' are the references to foreign rivalries limited to those with Russia, with no mention made of France and Germany?

(e) in the study of 'The Native Peoples of the Americas' is the study of North American Indians limited to those living in woods in the north eastern States?

(f) does the study of 'Britain in the Twentieth Century' stop at 1969 while studies of Europe, particularly Eastern Europe and Russia, of Black Africa and China reach well into the 1980s?

Incidentally, for a syllabus which seeks to anticipate change, why is there no mention of the Pacific? There is nothing about Australia, or South East Asia. Hong Kong gains a mention as part of the history of China. In studies of the United States virtually nothing of interest seems to have happened west of the Mississippi, and not much west of the Appalachians.

This is not an argument for adding to the number of required units or to the historical knowledge within them, indeed there still remains a strong case for considerably reducing them, nor is it suggested that the published History Study Units could not provide the basis for a sound history syllabus. However, there remains a powerful argument for a greater degree of choice between units, outside an agreed core, and for more flexibility within each individual unit. Such choices would:

(a) enable teachers to develop their own ideas;
(b) relate units to the regional and ethnic circumstances of individual schools;
(c) permit a variety of individual and group studies within one class which would be relevant to the 'experiences and background' and enthusiasms of the pupils;
(d) exemplify the Report's philosophy of teaching children that there is a variety of valid perspectives and interpretations of the past. Is not this attainment target contradicted by much of the prescriptive strategy of the Report?
(e) be more flexible and easily adaptable in anticipating changes in an often unpredictably changing world;
(f) be more consistent with the more flexible advice given by the Welsh History Committee to their Secretary of State.

A framework or map of the past

More choice, however, could increase somewhat the variety of gaps and reduce the chances of pupils leaving school at the age of 16 with a shared and common knowledge of key events in the past. Demands that pupils need this were often raised during the public debate on the place of history in schools. It was aired by Keith Joseph in his speech to the Historical Association in 1984 and discussed by HMI in *History in the Primary and Secondary Years* in 1985. There remains a strong argument for some kind of framework, time-line or map of the past to be built up during a pupil's school career which would grow out of the History Study Units but exist to one side of them. HMI argued the case that a framework or some form of time-line would help pupils 'define the chronological relationship of events and their relative distance from the present.' Such a time-line could become part of what has been termed 'a map of the past'. It would locate references not only to those periods and lives studied in detail but also to those receiving only cursory treatment. The knowledge and understanding of the events thus located would vary considerably, but understanding a map of the world does not mean equal knowledge of, say, the geography of Australia and that of Western Europe. It would, however, contain a skeleton of basic information, relate places to each other and establish a sense of scale. Similarly, a map of the past could not only provide pupils with a shared framework of knowledge but also serve as a reminder that people's lives and great occasions do not take place in isolation or out of context, and act as a systematic reminder that shared recognitions and memories help give communities – national, cultural, class – a claim to identity.

It probably does not really matter very much whether the basic features of the map are identical for all pupils. HMI offered three contrasted lists of basic features for consideration. *The Times Educational Supplement* asked five well known historians to compile their lists of key dates and events in British history. They were all different, valid and had considerable overlaps. But either there is going to be a series of suggested maps, or an official list, and the Report warns us of the dangers of that. Nor do I think we should be too fussed about whether children should or should not learn such a map by heart in a kind of Mastermind fashion. It is much more important that they understand what they are doing when they are compiling their map, that they should understand how the map could be refined and developed and in particular for what purposes it can be used.

What do the rationale and the History Study Units fail to mention?
There is no reference to or considered examination of, the historical concept of 'empathy'. During the very public debate about school history there was frequently expressed concern but often considerable misunderstanding about empathy, a misunderstanding once again repeated in *The Times Educational Supplement's* comments on the Report. Empathy and historical imagination refer to a particular kind of perspective about the past depending on evidence associated with some demanding skills. Merely to comment on the need to study other cultures through their eyes is too narrow and specific to provoke a useful discussion on this important issue. Scattered references in the Report to the need for 'a disciplined imagination' are too general and soft-centred. Presumably no one would seek to develop an *un*disciplined imagination! In any case it would be quite possible for a disciplined imagination, inspired by the past, to produce a painting, poem or piece of prose of genuine artistic and literary worth, but historically valueless. The important and sensitive issue of knowledge contained within its own attainment target received detailed and

persuasive consideration. The equally important and no less sensitive area of empathy and historical imagination justifies equally serious consideration.

The Schools History Project
The Report made one reference to the Project when it recognized its contribution to some of the valuable characteristics of GCSE and to much of the new thinking about school history. Nevertheless in 1989 some 63,145 candidates (27.2 per cent) sat a GCSE based on it. All of the Project schools and indeed many others have invested in Project material. Some of these could be used to support the teaching of a few HSUs. Others could not. The proposals for Key Stage 4 would not allow teachers to develop an SHP based examination course. We must assume that the ignoring and exclusion of the SHP represents the independent judgement of the Working Group, as no reference to the Project is made in its terms of reference. The many teachers who have taught it, and those who over the years developed, refined and implemented it, deserve much better.

Attainment targets and assessment
Like the PESC formula, attainment targets and assessment procedures are artificial constructs which are neither intrinsic to our perceptions of the past, nor in themselves a necessary part of developing historical skills, which incidentally have managed quite well up to now without this package of procedures and targets. They may be useful servants to help categorize ways of thinking about the past and, like PESC, potentially useful as *one* of the tools of initial planning and subsequent evaluation. The Report seems to recognize this by distinguishing between the content selected on 'historical grounds' and the four attainment targets selected on 'educational grounds . . . which reflect the intellectual growth of pupils', as when it writes 'assessment tasks should arise . . . from what is happening in the classroom and not be a separate or bolt-on on exercise', and, in relation to SATs, 'assessment must always, be the servant of teaching and learning, not the master.'

Attainment targets are seen particularly as a crucial part of complex and, possibly, very time-consuming, assessment procedures. It is important that there are as few targets as possible and that they seek to describe what real historians actually do. To have reduced the targets from five to four and gathered them under a single profile component of 'Historical Knowledge, Skills and Understanding' are undoubted gains over the recommendations in the Interim Report. The Institute of

Education and the National Association for History Advisers, suggested three targets: 'historical enquiry', 'explanation and understanding', and 'interpretation and accounts'; there seems no reason to revise these proposals. They would still contain some uncomfortable lacunae but three is better than four, and at least avoids the Report's misleading distinction between 'understanding points of view and interpretations of the past' and 'acquiring and *evaluating* historical information', and might help disentangle the assumed interdependent relation between the concepts of 'change and continuity' and 'cause and effect' contained within AT1.

The Working Group was asked 'to take account' of the TGAT proposals and 'offer advice in broad terms' on assessment. Apart from a statement, which earns our sympathy, 'that establishing a proper progression of historical understanding and skills over ten levels in an intelligible fashion is not an easy task', there is no evidence in the Report that the Group discussed the TGAT proposals. Assessment is such a crucial plank in the National Curriculum that it surely is inadequate for readers to have to assume that the TGAT proposals were accepted uncritically as applying to history. Was there no discussion, no unease? A difficult task is not necessarily impossible. A possible task does not have to be desirable or relevant to the need of history pupils and the adult world. *Are* there people in the adult world, in universities, business, the Civil Service who are measured on a ten-point scale and who need others so to be graded? Just *what* in society would be undermined by a simpler structure?

Having accepted an assessment strategy, how well is it executed in the Report? The introduction to the section on attainment levels listing the four attainment target recognizes that the development of children's understanding 'tends to be sporadic and uneven (we might add, frequently leap-frogs to unexpectedly high levels), that pupils can 'regress as well as progress' and that skills may not show in every context. This is all sound sense. A careful reading of the section seems to suggest that progress in historical understanding is 'inextricably bound to an increasingly sophisticated base of historical information' and not simply, it is noted, to an increasing *amount* of historical knowledge. The Report's introduction to the ranges of levels listing each attainment target offers useful summaries of progression. A reading of the 40 levels would provide many teachers with a programme for planning progression in teaching and learning, if, that is, they can be treated flexibly and not seen as a too rigid list of interdependent hierarchic stages. If however, the statutory instruments are precise and prescriptive flaws in the present wording of the levels will need to be ironed out. There are too many imprecisions and ambiguities, there are occasions when differences between levels lie in the wording rather than the difficulty of the activity, and there are even instances where demands in higher levels are, arguably, less than those at lower stages. More flexibility and fewer levels would only modify, not challenge, the essentials of the TGAT proposals.

There are some worrying passages about historical information and knowledge in which the Working Group seems nervily to be looking over its shoulder at ministerial attitudes and some pressure groups. For example the Report states: 'Teachers have an essential role to play in assessing pupils' acquisition of historical information as they teach each History Study Unit', and 'Historical Knowledge as information is important both for its own sake, and as a means of developing historical skills and understanding . . . We recommend therefore that SATs are always, and only, based on the essential historical information in programmes of study.' These statements seem once again to separate knowledge from a context of skills and understanding and unhelpfully to use the meaningless phrase 'knowledge for its own sake'. Such statements have to be read in the context of the whole Report, but they are not at this point sufficiently explained or qualified. They may well provide fuel for views against which the Report so persuasively argued more than a 100 pages earlier.

The Report has sensible recommendations on differentiation by outcome and by task. It recognizes that both strategies have problems and that neither has a monopoly of solutions, and its compromise recommendation is clear and practical: 'Our recommendation is therefore for a combination of tasks common to all pupils which would be assessed by outcome coupled with tasks which become progressively more difficult.' The Report adds, 'It is important that all pupils should have access to the same assessment tasks for their Key Stage, with no pre-determination or expectation of result'. Recommendations on weighting, aggregation and teacher assessment are also likely to attract much teacher support.

What the Report does not, and could not, do is to relate its recommendations to the realities of post-National Curriculum classrooms. They will present considerable planning tasks with related INSET needs. Final judgement must be reserved. The NCC and SEAC have much to do; the latter is charged particularly with re-examining the attainment targets, more especially the issue of the separate assessment of knowledge, and in the development of external tests,

Standard Assessment Tasks. It is hoped that future thinking will feel able to re-examine and publicly discuss the appropriateness of the TGAT strategy to history, and to think again about a too ready acceptance of ten levels of achievement.

All of these issues remind us that the implementation, evaluation and subsequent evolution of assessment procedures will have to be the result of a planned and costed partnership between the centre (DES, HMI, the NCC, SEAC) and teachers. Partners must be envisaged as more than carefully selected consultants. The Report after all pays tribute to teachers in the past who have designed 'new and improved forms of assessment.' How is this investment best realized in the future?

Resources and training

The Report defines resources as 'teachers, time and materials'. It makes a strong statement when it writes 'Current stocks of resources, current teaching expertise and current timetable assumptions will not, however, be sufficient to deliver the full range of our recommendations. Successful implementation cannot be achieved without adequate provision.' However it is understood that the Working Group's remit (although not publicly stated) did not encourage (or was it 'allow'?) their recommendations to be distracted or distorted by resource implications. So far ministerial responses have ignored this issue and concentrated on the problem of children learning facts. Whatever refinements the NCC and SEAC produce, they cannot increase resources for schools. Meanwhile ministerial timetables proceed serenely as if the problem did not exist.

The Report has, within its constraints, made some useful recommendations. It draws attention to a wide range of existing resources: information technology, historic sites, museums, literature, radio and TV, archives, oral history, archaeology. It states that visits should be seen as an integral part of the history curriculum and not just bolt-on treats. It does not, however, draw attention to the inhibiting regulations in the 1988 Education Reform Act concerning the charging of school visits, nor make any recommendations about their amendment. Nor does it draw attention to the accessible and often low-cost resource of the locality and region of the school. Greater use of these might throw into question the meagre donation of 17 per cent of time for School Designed Units in Key Stages 2 to 4, and the very prescriptive detail in them. Finally the Report does not highlight or even mention the existing and often ageing and decrepit resources in history stock-cupboards and on library shelves.

But there are suggestions which merit serious consideration and would benefit immensely from firm government backing. The Report

(a) recommends the appointment of a teacher to a primary school or to a cluster of schools with responsibility for developing the national curriculum in history. It is a strategy long supported by HMI and developed in many LEAs. It is unlikely to be wholly effective within existing financial limits and teacher-pupil ratios.

(b) attaches importance to the production of teaching materials in schools and commends teachers who 'have made an impressive contribution in the past to the design of syllabi, the production of resources, and the design of new and improved forms of assessment.' The contribution of teachers clearly has great merit. But the Report courteously ignores much that was poorly produced and unsuited to the needs of the pupils. Is it not just a little cool to commend past teacher initiatives when the proposed curriculum offers them little scope to develop them in the future? Here again for such initiatives to have significant impact on the learning of the new curriculum they will require more vigorous recognition by the DES of the profession-alism of teachers, backed by some resources of time and money.

(c) recommends a greater involvement of teachers with those in higher education, archivists and others, to produce resources. There are encouraging precedents: for example, the pioneering work with teachers by the School of Oriental and African Studies at the University of London; the development and evaluation of the Schools History Project; and, currently, two important initiatives for 16- to 18-year-olds – the Cambridge History Project (CHP) and the Enquiry into the Teaching of History to the Over Sixteens (ETHOS). None of these is cost-free either in terms of money or time.

The Report recognizes the INSET and initial training implications of much of this; the priorities it identifies are likely to make sense to teachers, teacher trainers, LEA advisers and HMI. It points out the needs of many primary teachers who will be teaching history for the first time, and of secondary teachers who will need to expand their existing knowledge base into new fields. The Report is sensitive to the considerable constraints within which teacher trainers work already, and, we might add, LEA advisers, HMIs and teachers. Other aspects of the Education Reform Act will add burdens to these groups without any prospect of their numbers being increased. That many will continue to strive and make do, often at considerable personal sacrifice, to assist in the training of teachers, is clear. But it is just too glib and cosy to shuffle off the problem by writing 'We are confident that new teachers will be trained sufficiently, and in time, to permit the successful implementation of our proposals.' Well it makes a good quote for ministers but will not entirely convince the profession.

The plot thickens: ministerial responses April to July 1990
In April 1990 Mrs Thatcher was interviewed in the *Sunday Telegraph*. She told her readers that she did not really feel that a prescribed syllabus 'should take up all the time devoted to that subject because you are going to lose the enthusiasm and devotion . . . that a really good teacher can give.' Just so, Prime Minister. She continued, 'Now the History Report has come out. It is very detailed . . . my worry is whether we should put out such a detailed one. You see, once you put out an approved curriculum, if you have got it wrong, the situation is worse afterwards than it was before. At any given time a large number of teachers are teaching a subject extremely well. But if you take them off what they know has worked for years, far better than anyone else's syllabus, then you wonder: were you doing it right?' Amen to that, Prime Minister. Apparently she shares, with the views expressed in this chapter, a concern about the level of prescription, as does Mr MacGregor who published his responses to the Final Report in July 1990.

In general he accepts the recommendations of the Final Report as a basis for his responses, but he asks for some significant alterations. They are concerned principally with the strategies for selecting and delivering HSUs and with the revision of the four proposed attainment targets.

The Secretary of State leaves the basic strategies of the HSUs intact but proposes to reduce 'the amount of real and apparent prescription' in them. This is a welcome move. Prescriptive detail listed under the headings of 'links', 'focus', 'concepts' and 'exemplary information' will be omitted. The National Curriculum Council is asked, although the wording of the response is not entirely clear on this point, to use the excluded material as the basis for *guidance* to teachers. The ambiguities of 'essential information' may now be reduced by being renamed 'content'. Mr MacGregor recognizes the concern over the sheer amount of content and detail in the proposed HSUs related to likely timetable allocation. But a reduction, by one, of the units in Key Stages 2 and 3 recognizes the problem without seriously grappling with it. He asks further whether some HSUs should be reduced in content, be less prescriptive and give teachers greater discretion in selecting content. In particular he proposes an important shift in emphasis in Key Stage 3. The four core units remain but teachers will be free in the four optional units to substitute a unit of their own choice, provided that they are consistent with the now more relaxed ground-rules and support the attainment targets. No changes affecting teacher choice are proposed for Key Stages 1, 2 and 4. The moves are in the right direction. Let them be welcomed, hoping that the NCC will make recommendations for their further extension.

The PESC formula is no longer to apply to optional units in Key Stage 2. It was a potentially useful formula if it was seen as simply one flexible tool in planning and evaluating the learning of the units. Not all its constituent categories had to be present all the time. Nil returns would have been welcome and often historically appropriate. But the formula can act as a reminder that important aspects of the past had often been ignored: scientific and technological and cultural developments in particular. The absence of PESC or its equivalent may be seen to offer a life-line to those teachers who still lazily limit their views of the past to political, diplomatic and, sometimes, economic, factors.

Proposed changes in Key Stage 4 are of a different kind and somewhat odder. Two core units remain but they are to be considerably broadened. Their scope now boggles the mind. One is to be called 'Twentieth Century World History, including the Second World War.' The other is on 'Twentieth Century Britain', and there are a further two on other aspects of European and World history and finally a School Designed Unit covering at least five hundred years of British History. It all adds up to an average of one major unit per term. Surely some mistake? A misprint perhaps? Not tired and emotional writing we can be sure. Alas not. Raising standards seems to have become confused with increasing perspiration. Will the NCC be able to produce a teachable examination syllabus which further develops the skills and insights already acquired, and be able at the same time to meet the high and realistic criteria of SEAC?

Those pupils who may follow a reduced course in Key Stage 4 remain excluded from studying an SDU and there is still cold comfort for those schools who have taught, and have the resources for, the Schools History Project. Are the availability of the resources and the growing popularity of a syllabus to be dismissed, or rather ignored, as valid criteria for selection?

Equally fundamental, and perhaps more controversial, is Mr MacGregor's response on attainment targets. He proposes to reduce these from four to three. ATs 2 and 3, 'Understanding Points of View and Interpretations of History' and 'Acquiring and Evaluating Historical Information', remain. AT 4, 'Organizing and Communicating the Results of Historical Study' is abandoned as its skills are not unreasonably seen as necessarily permeating all the other targets. A new Attainment Target 1 is proposed to be called 'Knowledge and Understanding'.

Immediate press reaction to this response was to see it as a victory for the traditionalists (there were references to 'grim smiles of satisfaction') over the advocates of the New History and to relate it to a debate nurtured by, and more apparent in, newspaper columns than detectable in history classrooms. The Final Report distinguished three uses of the word 'knowledge': *knowledge as information* 'basic facts, for example, names, dates, events'; *knowledge as content* 'the subject matter of history, for example, a period or a theme'; *knowledge as understanding* 'facts studied in relation to other facts and evidence about them, and placed in an explanatory framework which enables their significance to be perceived'. It is this last use of the term that is most germane to Mr MacGregor's response. How should we react to it? How might it be interpreted by the NCC so as to make sense in classrooms, and avoid patronizing children and lowering standards by increasing rote-learning? Has this proposal seriously undermined and contradicted the careful and persuasive arguments deployed in the Final Report against the isolation of knowledge into its own attainment target?

In the first place 'understanding' is a helpfully imprecise term, as is the Final Report's definition of it. Its use in the new Attainment Target 1 makes it clear that knowledge is *not* being separated from its context or from the kind of evidence which authenticates it. References to perceiving significance encompass a clutch of questions and skills concerned with the analysis and applicability of knowledge and pose the questions 'Significant for whom? For what purpose?' Thus new AT 1 could properly be interpreted as necessarily concerned with knowledge in context and with the simultaneous and not subsequent acquisition of necessary skills. We do not know whether the NCC will interpret it in this way but if they do it would not be inconsistent either with the recommendations, or with the rest of the Final Report which Mr MacGregor accepts.

In the second place the Report makes an important statement which deserved to have been developed and given much more prominence. The Report wrote 'Assessment tasks should arise ... from what is happening in the classroom and not be separate or bolt-on exercises' and, in relation to Standard Assessment Tasks (SATs) 'must always be the servant of teaching and learning not the master'. The Report also points out that not all HSUs are capable of delivering equally all attainment targets. So the Report's recommendations mean that separate attainment targets, which are after all artificial constructs on which the learning of history does not in itself depend, should *not* be seen as representing separate assessment exercises. Thus it must follow that they cannot necessarily represent separate teaching strategies. It follows, for example, that the separate teaching of knowledge is neither recommended nor apparently required.

Is there nothing then to worry about in this recommendation? There remain three concerns. The first is that the Secretary of State recommends higher weighting for his new Attainment Target 1. This is against the wise advice of the Final Report which concluded that: 'There was no compelling theoretical or practical basis for applying different weightings (to attainment targets). If pupils responded to a question in terms of a lower-weighted attainment target then they could be disadvantaged if they had unwittingly emphasised this attainment target. We therefore recommend that the attainment targets and the strands within them be given equal weight.'

Why then did Mr MacGregor reject this advice? Because, as he says, 'The mastery of knowledge seems to me to measure most directly what pupils have learned from their historical studies'. Perhaps it is *easier* to measure the acquisition of knowledge, though it is dubious whether knowing more can in any sensible way be related to levels of attainment. Even the partnership of 'knowledge and understanding' does not effectively dispose of the sensible words of the Final Report on weighting, based as they are on how real classes work and pupils learn. Mr MacGregor's words seem to suggest that assessment, on this point anyway, has become the master not the servant of learning.

Further, the original proposal saw knowledge as a necessary basis for the skills and understanding in *all* attainment targets. There has been much publicly expressed concern about process-led or dominated curricula, sometimes caricatured as 'provided the skills are right the knowledge does not matter'. However, the separation of knowledge into its own attainment target may well be seen as tacitly supporting, in Attainment Targets 2 and 3, the development of skills *without* knowledge. Surely the best way to ensure that a curriculum is not skills-dominated but rather skills-supported is to ensure that knowledge permeates all ATs as a necessary part of all historical learning?

Finally the Secretary of State has seen fit not only to reject the Working Group's recommendation on weighting but also its careful argument against the separation of knowledge into a separate AT. This view received very widespread professional support as, for example, the evidence from the Historical Association summarizing views expressed at its series of regional conferences. In April 1990 the Secretary of State asked SEAC to advise him on the assessment of knowledge within attainment targets. Its reply is published and is part of the documentation sent by Mr MacGregor to the NCC. SEAC comments, sometimes critically, always positively, on the Final Report but they 'accept the History Working Group's position that information and content should only be specified in the programmes of study', i.e. not in attainment targets. Mr MacGregor seems seriously to seek professional opinion. But on this issue he does not so much argue against the weight of experienced and carefully argued opinion, he simply ignores it. Is professional advice sought in order to influence policy, or to provide an agenda for discussion, or merely to confirm existing political attitudes?

The Final Report's comments on inadequate resources and on the need for new and sustained programmes of inservice and initial teacher training are acknowledged by the Secretary of State. His response is 'These (recommendations) will be duly considered with any comments on them'. The ability to teach and learn the new curriculum and effectively to resource it will depend, from the outset, on some specific reassurances about resources. Deft sweepings under the carpeted corridors of the 12th Floor of Elizabeth House are on this key issue simply not good enough.

In sum, Mr MacGregor's responses are a rum mix. In part they are more sensitive to the experience of teachers and their current difficulties and will enable some more HSUs to reflect available resources, local and regional circumstances and the social and ethnic mix in classrooms. There is evidence that Mr MacGregor is a listener increasingly aware of the colossal problems raised by implementing the National Curriculum. But our applause must remain cautious, tempered by his other views which are a disconcerting and sometimes batty mixture of nerviness and obstinacy. However the National Curriculum Council may yet provide an honourable and professionally acceptable route back to complete sanity.

Conclusion: the future
In sum, we have a Report whose recommendations provide a base for professional acceptance, from some of whose incidental sillinesses Mr MacGregor has saved it. It is not yet, nor does it claim to be, a usable working document, but it has earned the right to be influential. It has

its own historical context. It is the product of, and will be moulded and redirected by, change.

If the Report seeks to remain loyal to its own philosophy there are presumably alternative perspectives and interpretations to its view of the past. However some further shift in emphasis in its proposals to increase choice and to simplify the assessment procedures would leave the case for a national curriculum intact and in no way undermine its rationale for history in schools. A shift would also enable the Report to mean what it says when it writes, 'the content of a history course requires constant evaluation and almost certainly regular re-casting', and avoid a possible contradiction when it recommends, soon after, that the basic structure should 'endure for some years.' Over-centralized schemes sometimes require softening with some degree of market economy.

Most educational and curricular choices are not made because truth has been monopolized or the philosopher's stone discovered. Rather they are a pragmatic recognition of untidy compromise and a need to choose the particular disadvantages we have to live with. In an open and pluralist society which encourages, in the words of the Report, 'the development of the quality of open-mindedness which questions assumptions and demands evidence for points of view', we must surely opt for the untidiness and unpredictability of more choice based on declared criteria. It would be ironic if the questioning of assumptions and demands for evidence for points of view applied to the primary source called *History Working Group: Final Report*, were to find it wanting. The Final Report and some of the ministerial responses to it have too many virtues for their flaws to be allowed to decline into mortal wounds.

Postscript: 31st July 1990

On 31st July the Secretary of State spoke to the Professional Association of Teachers. The views he expressed have also been sent to the National Curriculum Council for their consideration. They blow a discrete post-parliamentary session summer season fanfare signalling a major retreat from some of the aims of the National Curriculum. It can been seen as further recognition by Mr MacGregor that a hurriedly ill-conceived National Curriculum announced by his predecessor on his way through Elizabeth House was unteachable. So Mr MacGregor has raised the possibility of essential subjects like art, music, and P.E. being dropped and that history and geography may once again become alternatives or combined in a joint course. The great venture may be about to founder at the outset.

Lack of resources and teachers, unforeseen burdens of testing and assessment, do not in any way lessen the crucial importance of historical education for all young people aged five to 16. It is not surprising, nor dishonourable, to recognize that the National Curriculum would have growing pains and unanticipated difficulties. Mr MacGregor has shown that he wants a much more flexibly interpreted and less prescriptive history curriculum, but there are no signs yet of a frank admission that resources at present are inadequate, of announcing their increase as a desirable mid- and long-term aim, or of accepting a more flexible timetable for implementation. The sacrifices he announced in late July are essential components in children's learning and not in the parliamentary timetable. The *Independent* wrote in a leader on the 2nd of August: (Mr MacGregor) 'threatens history, widely accepted as one of the fundamentals of a good basic education. He is approaching that ill-defined line beyond which pragmatic flexibility becomes a retreat from essentials.'

There is much professional and bipartisan support for the Final Report and, I suspect, for many of the Secretary of State's responses to it. Political timetables surely should not be allowed to determine a curriculum which not only seeks to raise standards but to define what all young people are entitled to gain from their years of compulsory education.

Now we must look to the professional judgement of the NCC and SEAC. With them rest some central questions. Do we want a professional teaching force? Have we got one? If not, how best do we identify, recognize and promote it? Do the proposals of the National Curriculum and the Secretary of State assist in the process? If not, much of the task of developing that professionalism rests with SEAC and the NCC. Meanwhile, out there, the teachers of history wait, with their experience, to make *their* contribution as partners to the process. They know that in the end the success of the whole enterprise depends on them.

Chapter Three
Historical Knowledge and the National Curriculum

Peter Lee

A National Curriculum is under construction, and history is to be part of it. There is widespread agreement among teachers and historians that this is a welcome development. Some headteachers may try to squeeze history or seek hybrid 'humanities' approaches, but the Government's intention is that history will be taught for three or four periods a week up to the age of 14, and for 'a reasonable time' until 16. (Schools which fail to offer all the National Curriculum subjects at GCSE are not likely to do well in an environment dominated by LMS, parent governors, and competition based on published results.) History must be learnt in school. But what does this actually mean?

Knowing about the past
Whatever else it means, learning history must mean learning about the past, and this implies that history teaching is – among other things – handing on a knowledge of the past. Unfortunately this is the point at which the apparent unanimity of politicians, teachers and historians collapses. Is handing on knowledge of the past to be understood as:

(a) something to be acquired for its own sake – as intrinsically valuable or enjoyable, or as part of what it is to be educated;
(b) knowledge which enables pupils to understand human behaviour better (both past and present), perhaps requiring detailed particular knowledge;
(c) background information required for understanding present concerns (often construed as 'problems');
(d) knowledge relevant to children's needs and/or concerns;
(e) socially important knowledge (concepts of what to include will

differ: examples frequently offered are 'the growth of British
democracy' and 'the development of a multicultural society');
(f) part of a common heritage;
(g) something which creates or reinforces patriotism or pride in 'our'
history;
(h) a framework or map of the past?

It is immediately obvious that what looks like one common-sense
approach to school history is in fact a plethora of different approaches,
united only by the misleadingly self-evident view that schoolchildren
learning history should do just that: learn what happened in the past.
Unfortunately 'learning what happened' is problematic on at least two
counts: not everything that happened can be learnt (not least because
the notion of 'everything that happened' is an incoherent one) and
agreement on what happened is not guaranteed. The consequences of
these problems are most serious for those versions of the 'knowledge of
the past' approach which most explicitly go beyond history in search of
social and political goals.

The idea of handing on a common heritage offers a clear example of
the difficulties. There was in the past no consensus as to how to live.
Which heritage is to be selected? What should be said about the
different traditions within British life (even without taking into account
those heritages belonging to communities established in Britain as a
result of immigration)? Historians disagree about the role in British life
of those traditions, let alone their historical significance. But what is at
issue is not simply a matter of disagreement in historians' assumptions.
Politicians who wish to announce the demise of particular traditions
which they find uncongenial may find it hard to understand that the
past changes as the future alters what may be said about it, but this is
the nature of history. It is shown in every area from population change
or political upheaval to the impact of technology. What was said about
the significance of the British nuclear power programme in the late
1950s, what can be said now, and what it will be possible to say in 50 or
100 years' time are all very different, as will be obvious if the phrases
'was the beginning of', 'was the precursor of', and 'was the cause of' are
considered. We cannot say now that the 1950s saw the beginning of an
energy technology which allowed the worst consequences of the
greenhouse effect to be avoided without major economic penalties, or
alternatively that it caused large-scale economic problems as a result of
massive environmental pollution; but it is possible that either, neither or
both of these statements could be justifiably asserted in 50 years' time.

The same changes occur in the assessment of cherished institutions, hallowed individuals and *a fortiori* of traditions as components of heritages. Handing on a common heritage is nothing to do with learning history: it is using the past for practical social and political ends. This kind of practical past is not necessarily illegitimate, but it is not to be confused with history.

These considerations apply even more clearly in the case of imparting knowledge of the past in order to create or reinforce patriotism or pride in 'our' history, an approach which runs counter to criteria of detachment and impartiality built into genuine historical study. Once again it is important to stress that to say this is to say nothing about the legitimacy of attempting to create patriotic children, merely about the relationship of this kind of activity to teaching and learning history.

There has always been a tension in school history between those who see learning history as an end in itself, and those who see it as a means to further ends. It is too easy to produce sets of politically appealing dichotomies. The present fashion is to juxtapose 'history for its own sake' with 'relevance'. Relevance is an imprecise notion in debates about history teaching: appeals to relevance need explicit criteria, together with a statement spelling out to whom or to what history should be relevant. The usual sleight of hand here is to move from the unexceptionable premise that children should feel that what they are being asked to learn has some value to them, to the (usually) tacit claim that what children do not immediately recognize as directly connected with their concerns or experience cannot be of value to them. This leads to narrowing and damaging consequences in history, where the same basic line of argument is, somewhat paradoxically, used to prescribe on the one hand very recent 'world history', and on the other a span of British history. The claim in one case is that pupils want and need knowledge of recent events in an increasingly interdependent world, and in the other that if they are British, they will want and need knowledge of the past of their own society. Claims of this kind usually rest on anecdotal evidence, for the excellent reason that no one has acquired serious evidence. Nor do claims about pupils' needs have much to do with criteria intrinsic to learning history, but are better understood as either appealing to wider educational goals, or directly to social purposes. Those who wish to change society through history teaching in one direction are sometimes accused of social engineering. Those who wish to change it in another, or who strive to prevent change, are clearly no mean engineers in their own right. Neither group deserves any credence in serious discussion of school history, because the basis of their proposals lies in political concerns extrinsic to teaching history. Socialization, the creation of confident patriots or even of 'good citizens' (a spuriously neutral phrase usually devoid of explicit substantive content) cannot justify handing on knowledge of the past or determine how it is done, because these goals are contested slogans, not appeals to historical criteria.

'History for its own sake' is one of those slogans which has managed both to acquire a bad name in schools and at the same time to remain obscure. Its obscurity is partly to blame for its bad name, because in one of its possible meanings it makes a great deal of sense. Some teachers have regarded the assertion that history should be studied for its own sake as both élitist and absurd. The assumption was that studies in school must be *useful* (in much the same way as technology is useful) and that studying something for its own sake is an admission that it is not useful but merely *academic*, and hence something which can have value only for an élite, or as a means of marking off and preserving an élite. It may be that some advocates of 'history for its own sake' believe that history is the exclusive preserve of a leisured élite, but such a view is not a necessary consequence of taking the position that history should be studied for itself.

There are more serious arguments at issue here. Implicit in the case for studying history for its own sake is the reminder that the past is used for every kind of practical purpose by lawyers, clergymen, politicians and journalists. Such uses are not automatically illegitimate, but the practical past is not the historical past.[1] Organizing the past to enable it to answer our current practical concerns is not doing history. History is not a practical subject: it has no skills or lessons which can be directly *applied* in clearly defined activities or to neatly demarcated classes of physical objects. What is learnt in history is not useful in the way technology or (potentially applied) science is useful. Technology and some kinds of science are useful as means to ends, and although politicians and businessmen disagree profoundly about ends, they can all subscribe to the importance of means without damaging their pursuit of whatever ends they have in mind. History changes our whole view of the world, of what the present is and of what human beings are and might be, and in so doing has the potential to change ends. This, as political leaders are quick to recognize, is dangerous.[2] At the same time the past is inescapable: in different ways it is built into the present in our physical and social concepts. (For something to be a scar or a crater, certain events must have taken place; and similarly concepts like father-in-law or elected government are only valid if certain events or processes have occurred in the past.) Our understanding of policies (appeasement, socialism, Gaullism), or of what particular nations are and may become, depends on our understanding of their past; and the same is true of institutions like political parties, trade unions, banks and manufacturing companies. Ignorance of the past is, in this sense, ignorance of the present. The discipline of history offers a rational past, not merely a practical one designed to suit the interests of particular groups or kinds of activity.[3] It is rational because it incorporates public criteria and operates through open procedures. These do not guarantee truth, but they do make the discipline a serious attempt to produce the best account we can, given the state of our questioning and the evidence available. In this sense objectivity (as opposed to partiality or vicious relativism) is built into the discipline of history.

The claim that history should be studied for its own sake is, then, a way of making two assertions: that history is not useful as a means to an end, but valuable as something which expands our whole picture of the world and of what ends might be possible; and that to have this value it must be genuine history, not the practical past in disguise. The reason for teaching history in school is not so that pupils can use it for making something else, or to change or preserve a particular form of society, or even to expand the economy. The reason for teaching history is not that it changes society, but that it changes *pupils*; it changes what they see in the world, and how they see it. It can only do this if it *is* history, not a piece of the past convenient to use for some short-term 'national interest', political ambition or educational fashion. It must not present the myths against which Kitson Clark so elegantly warned us more than two decades ago.[4]

> From [a] haphazard mass of misty knowledge, scraps of information, fiction in fancy dress and hardly conscious historical memories is woven a network of historical associations which stretches over the whole field of human consciousness. Thus words are converted into spells, symbols are endowed with emotional force and stereotypes emerge . . . Here in fact are some of the most powerful forces which control the human mind. They are of much use to those who wish to invoke irrational loyalties.[5]

Handing on knowledge of the past only makes educational sense if what is handed on is real *historical* knowledge. Acceptance of this proposition can lead in two different directions, culminating at their extremes in very different points of view. In the first view genuine historical

knowledge is no more and no less than the certified facts: certified, that
is, by historians. Learning about the past at school means learning a
selection of those facts. The second view insists that real historical
knowledge involves knowing what constitutes 'good grounds' for
claims to knowledge in history. This means that learning about the past
means learning about the discipline too. These two positions represent
the ends of a continuum along which various intermediate positions are
possible. They are not synonymous with 'traditional' and 'new' history,
but the difference in emphasis which they enshrine is central to any
attempt to characterize those two labels.

The primacy of fact
The view that genuine historical knowledge to be taught in school can
only be the certified facts is a persuasive one. There is a temptation
among 'plain thinking' people to make strong statements about the
necessity for pupils to know the facts, and about the futility of
attempting much else in school history. This is often asserted as a truism
which needs no justification, but is sometimes supported by the claim
that pupils can only explain, analyse or evaluate anything in history
after they have acquired the facts. There are major difficulties with this
simple, no-nonsense view, two of which will be considered here.

Specifying the facts
The first serious difficulty in the view that children must know a certain
corpus of facts is that it is extemely difficult to specify what they should
be. This is not a point about problems of selection, but about
confusions as to the nature of historical fact. Those who assert that
children must know the facts tend to offer lists of events and dates,
names of people, and the names of colligations like 'The Reformation'.
A list of this kind does not amount to a statement of what facts should
be learnt by pupils. Facts – speaking plainly, if crudely – are what true
statements state. 'Nelson', 'The battle of Trafalgar', and 'The Reformation' are not statements in which something is asserted, and in
consequence cannot be true or false. They do not say anything about
the past, or impart knowledge or understanding, or amount to anything
coherent or even intelligible. To do any of these things, they must be
placed in a proposition in which something is asserted. This is why the
lists of names and concepts in the History Study Units offered by the
Final Report of the History Working Group do not, for all their
detailed prescription, actually amount to a specification of facts to be
learnt.[6]

Were such a specification attempted it might take either of two forms. It could be a set of statements or, rather more sophisticated, a list of dates with statements following them, perhaps – using material from the Report – something like this:

> 1805 AD. A great battle between the British fleet and the French and Spanish fleets was fought at Trafalgar, and the British had the victory.
>
> 1812 AD. The Emperor Napoleon collected a great army and invaded the lands of the Russian Tsar.

Alternatively, the specification might consist of facts linked together in such a way as to form an account. There are, of course, important questions lurking here about the relationship between annals, chronicle and narrative, but for the purposes of this paper it is enough to mark the distinction between tables of discrete factual statements on one hand and accounts on the other.[7]

The point is a simple one: any attempt to specify the facts which children should learn will either lapse into something very similar to annals, and rightly be subject to ridicule; or it will be an account of some kind. But the latter is a jump from the frying pan into the fire: what democratic government in its right mind is going to lay down *the* account of the past which children must learn? The experience of authoritarian dictatorships of every colour makes such a step to Party history inconceivable, quite apart from the fact that it would be in direct conflict with the nature of the discipline.

However, if history has its own standards, and a real claim to objectivity, where is the danger in giving children 'the best account' we can get at the moment? The trouble is there is never just one 'best account', because there is never just one question. The objectivity of history is relative to the questions asked. To say this is *not* to say that any old account will do, or that choosing between accounts is merely a matter of political taste or determined by social interests. It does not involve a slide into vicious relativism, or into subjectivism: on the contrary, given a certain question there may be only one best answer. Even questions have to meet standards – some are uninteresting and some merely foolish. The community (or communities) of historians often share a large measure of agreement about what questions are worth asking at any particular moment, because they share explanatory ideals which change rather slowly. But they agree only within a range, and at any given moment the questions worth asking constitute an open set, and the accounts which may be constructed to answer them are correspondingly numerous and heterogeneous. Historians agree not on one story, but on the parameters within which several stories are valid.

All this means that the demand for a history curriculum in which the facts are specified collapses into absurdity. In a democratic society a history curriculum cannot specify the facts: it can merely specify the topics to be studied. (Note that this does *not* amount to specifying the facts by the back door, only the area in which facts are to be learnt.) Specification of topics is very different from specification of facts: a demand for *rigour* can turn out to be a demand for *control* over what is held to be important, whether this is determined by historical criteria, or by political and social goals. Few attempts have been made to set out historical criteria of importance and it is hard to see how they could determine content in any close or detailed way.[8] Historical criteria allow a great deal of room for manoeuvre, but politicians may well have their own reasons for restricting it. Nevertheless, if what is at issue is the rigorous study of history, political and social goals must be clearly distinguished from and remain firmly subordinate to genuine historical criteria.

The paradox here is that a demand which derives from a concern that rigorous historical standards should be maintained in schools leads easily into a position the practical consequence of which is unhistorical political mythologizing. This is precisely why many of the best 'traditional' history teachers (in grammar, direct-grant and independent as well as comprehensive schools) moved back in the late 1960s and early 1970s to a position similar to the one advocated by Keatinge in 1910, in which understanding the discipline was of central importance.[9] The textbooks and examinations with which they had been operating had turned history into socializing mythology (a perversion of history which is politically colour-blind).[10]

In short, the common-sense claim that children should learn neither more nor less than the certified facts is not false, but simplistic and misleading. Of course pupils learning history must learn about the past, and of course this means they must learn facts. But this is not an argument that those who write the history curriculum must specify the facts. *That* demand cannot be supported by truisms, and is in any case confused, misleading and ultimately dangerous. The Report of the History Working Group does not attempt such a thing, and NCC and SEAC must not allow themselves to be pushed into attempting it.[11]

First the facts, then the thinking

Another difficulty with assertions of the absolute primacy of certified facts is that they confuse logic and psychology. It is true that a pupil cannot explain why something happened unless, in some sense, he or she knows what *did* happen. But pupils do not function in the way this neat little 'common-sense' statement suggests. Learning what happened and why it happened go on together in the real world of the classroom, because children do not switch off their attempts to make sense of the world until a teacher, professor or politician tells them they now know enough to start thinking. Moreover, even if logical presupposition automatically dictated temporal order, there would be no decision procedure for determining when the facts were sufficient to allow explanation to begin.

Pupils have ideas. These ideas may seem risible or mistaken or inconsequential to politicians and professional historians, but to professional teachers they are of central importance. The assumption that it is possible to pass on the facts, and only later develop ideas to make sense of them is not only conceptually naive, it is empirically false. Any comment on what can or should be taught in school history which is ignorant of the available evidence of children's ideas invites treatment as amateur speculation, or worse as empty pontification.[12] Pupils continuously attempt to make sense of what they encounter, and the assumptions and tacit understandings with which they operate are a major determinant of what they make of the history presented to them. Pupils' ideas may be flawed, but a deficit approach fails to come to terms with the fact that they are positive attempts to order the historical world (both the discipline and what it produces). They are not equally effective: some ideas work better in a wider range of circumstances than others. The teacher must discover and address the ideas pupils are operating with, and try to replace the weaker ones with more effective ones. These goals take time to achieve, which is why it is important not to overload the history curriculum with too many topics.

Since learning history involves learning about the past, teaching history necessarily involves handing on facts, but this is not enough. If pupils are to learn genuine history they will need to understand how the discipline works, about the basis of historical knowledge, and about what marks off the historical from the practical past. Even a copious supply of historically established facts is an inadequate diet for children, partly as a consequence of the nature of history, and partly because pupils are not passive receptacles who are brought to history with no ideas of their own. History is more than the sum of its discrete facts: a story composed entirely of true statements may be totally misleading, and in any case there is never just one story. Pupils have tacit understandings about the discipline of history, just as they do about its substance, and teaching which ignores these will simply be building ambitious structures on unexamined and shifting foundations.

Learning the discipline
There are logical and practical reasons for insisting that pupils must know something more than past facts, even if the latter are understood as part of an account. In the first place, the idea of knowledge itself imposes certain standards. It is generally held that if I can be said to *know* something, I have good grounds for what I believe. Plainly it would be foolish to push this claim too far. Historians happily (and necessarily) rely on assertions made by their colleagues in their professional capacity. No professional historian could conceivably have good grounds for every assertion if this meant that he or she had personally to examine all the evidence relevant to each assertion. Are not pupils in a similar, if more extreme, position?

A historian can accept colleagues' work as knowledge because those colleagues have been trained in sets of shared procedures and standards, and their work has been subjected to the scrutiny of professionals. The standards and procedures will be realized in the way assertions are justified in argument, in the marshalling and display of evidence, and in the maintenance of a degree of detachment and impartiality. The apparatus of citation, bibliography and footnotes, employed where appropriate, will be a public invitation and opportunity to test the claims to knowledge at any point. All this presupposes that historians understand and accept the procedures and standards involved in the discipline.

Children coming fresh to school history know nothing of this. When pupils learn the products of historians' research, they still do not know any history unless they understand something of what counts as good grounds. They cannot be historians (if 'historian' means 'professional historian') and it would be absurd to insist that pupils test everything they are taught by direct recourse to the relevant sources, let alone produce all their history from the sources themselves. It is equally absurd, however, to say that schoolchildren know any history if they have no understanding of how historical knowledge is attained, its relationship to evidence, and the way in which historians arbitrate between competing or contradictory claims. The ability to recall accounts without any understanding of the problems involved in constructing them or the criteria involved in evaluating them has nothing historical about it. Without an understanding of what makes an account historical, there is nothing to distinguish such an ability from the ability to recite sagas, legends, myths or poems.

All this, of course, begs difficult questions about the extent to which and the way in which we can talk of accounts being true. It is said there is much agreement, even consensus, in history about the best or the 'standard work' on a particular passage of history or historical topic. There is some truth in this, but it remains a half-truth, concealing as much as it reveals. The fact that it is used as an argument in discussion of school history indicates a certain degree of condescension towards pupils: there is enough agreement for children, who after all understand little about the world. (Perhaps it also testifies to condescension towards teachers, who, despite their undergraduate studies, cannot be trusted to get their history right.)

Even were the half-truth acceptable, it would not support the weight put upon it. The 'standard work' may be a multifaceted piece of history, interweaving multiple strands, linking complementary interpretations, interrelating different questions, and moving between different perspectives. Is it seriously suggested that *this* is what children should learn? The same pupils who are held not to be able to cope with anything except a single account are now to be faced with an immensely complex and sophisticated structure. Plainly this is not what the school consensus view intends. The move from a professional consensus to a single account is evidently a sleight of hand.

But *which* account is licensed by the standard work. Either we are back to annals, or to *the* account.[13] Pupils must learn facts, and the facts they learn must be understood. This means they must be related to one another in legitimate ways, frequently in the form of an account. But *just one* account would be hopelessly unhistorical, artificial and sterile, and it would be in practice almost impossible to shield children from conflicting accounts. It is also unnecessary.[14] Once it is accepted that knowledge implies understanding of the grounds for historical claims, the problem ceases to be one of constructing an anodyne all-purpose account, and becomes one of enabling children to understand why it is possible to have different accounts, and how those accounts must meet certain standards.

This may seem a tall order for schoolchildren. Interpreted as meaning that pupils must reach the level of professional historians, such a goal is wildly inappropriate. It is hard to see how anyone could imagine that teachers could seriously entertain this interpretation. The acquisition of understanding is not an all-or-nothing achievement. It seems unlikely that the Secretary of State for Education has the same grasp of the nature of and reasons for disagreement among historians as do professional historians themselves, but this is not to say that he has no clue whatsoever about such matters, or even that he has no more understanding than a ten-year-old. There may even be gradations of understanding among historians, and there is certainly evidence for variations of this kind among teachers. If this is accepted, then what is at issue is not a choice between acceptance or rejection of absurdly grandiose goals, but decisions as to the level of understanding it is reasonable to aim for in this area with pupils of particular ages, and the desirability of spending time and effort in pursuing such goals.

Two kinds of reservations might arise at this juncture: that it is undesirable for some reason to try to develop children's understanding of why historians produce differing accounts, and that it is simply not possible in practice to achieve worthwhile attainments here. Presumably no one would argue that the goal is simply undesirable *tout court*. This leaves us with the second reservation. The matter is not entirely an empirical one, because the criteria for what is to count as a worthwhile achievement cannot be fixed empirically, but it is not an armchair problem either. There is considerable empirical evidence available in a variety of forms. Classroom practitioners, examination boards, researchers, and HMI all agree that major gains in children's understanding can be achieved.[15] Perhaps even this is not enough, because any simplification of the understandings involved might be thought to be dangerous. This could mean that it must lead children to hold other sets of dangerous beliefs (some kind of vicious relativism, for example), or that it is somehow intrinsically dangerous (possibly in the sense of necessarily consisting of half-truths and therefore being untrue to history). Once again the first caveat is an empirical matter: it seems more likely that relativism is a product of the disillusionment caused by unprepared encounter with unimagined conflicts among historians than something engendered by courses designed to emphasize that history has public criteria and to help students understand them – but this is not something that can be decided on a priori grounds. The second caveat is illuminating, because it seems to suggest that while it makes no difference to anything important if children leave school with a highly simplified (distorted?) understanding of substantive history, they cannot safely be allowed simplified second-order understandings. This is particularly curious in that this sort of argument is generally coupled with assertions about the importance of *real* history as opposed to mere methodological 'exercises'. However, could it be that a better grasp of the way the discipline works, even if highly simplified, will enable pupils to make more sense of real history?

Learning history is difficult, and does not take place in a flash at 18 or even at 25. It is a gradual process of developing ideas, in which pupils need a great deal of help. A substantial part of what is learnt has to be *knowing-how*, not just *knowing-that*. Some of what children have to learn is not in itself historical knowledge at all, but provides both crutches and tools for assisting them to acquire that knowledge.

What must history teach in school?
Practising teachers, examiners, researchers, LEA inspectors and HMI have gradually come to believe that teaching history requires the sharpest specification of targets that is possible and appropriate. This has been a practical consensus, based on what is most effective in promoting learning, on what teachers need to ensure their efficiency in an under-resourced system, and on what is required for reliable and valid assessment. Any categorization of the different elements which make up school history is likely to offer misleading messages, if only the very obvious one that it cuts the fabric of history into pieces. The set of categories employed in what follows is based on one particular set of assumptions, and is to be regarded simply as a device for the purposes of this discussion.[16]

Dispositions
Learning history is learning 'standards', but learning standards is more than knowing that something is the case, or how to do something, or even how something ought to be done. It is acquiring a disposition to behave in certain ways. Commitment to truth, respect for the past (however strange and unsympathetic it may seem) and impartiality are built into learning history. If pupils do not learn these, they have not even begun to understand history. It is possible that these standards will be 'picked up' by pupils as they learn about the past without receiving any explicit attention, but experience suggests that teaching and learning will be more effective if pupils are made explicitly aware of the standards and principles at the root of the study of history. In the last resort it is the teacher's practical commitment to the principles which is decisive: exhortation will have little effect. But it may be easier to learn principles by example if, at least at some point, they have been spelt out. No one has seriously investigated this area yet, despite its importance. We simply do not know whether children acquire even a minimal

respect for truth as they learn history (or indeed science or geography). On the other hand there is increasing evidence that pupils can and do acquire *some* understanding of the procedures which give substance to the principle.

Structural concepts

Pupils have tacit understandings of what constitutes an historical fact, of what counts as an adequate explanation of actions or events, and of what can legitimately give sense to the changes they encounter in passages of the past. These understandings may, from the perspective of the professional historian, be risibly inadequate, just as the understandings acquired by that same historian in other academic or practical spheres – for example in particle physics or electrical wiring – may be correspondingly inadequate from the standpoint of the professional. But the ability to install a simple ring main is an immense improvement over defeat in the face of fitting a plug. Our hypothetical historian may have no aspirations in fundamental physics, but be much better equipped to understand the physical world and changing technological possibilities if he or she has grasped even an entirely non-mathematical (and hence misleading and distorting) exposition of relativity and quantum theory. More important, our historian's notion of what constitutes a scientific theory, or of the role of experiment in science, may evolve from ideas going little beyond the glorified cookery of one kind of school science to an understanding which, while still partial and mistaken, allows him or her to make sense of the whole enterprise of science and its continuing achievements.

The second-order concepts with which children operate in learning history at school are of central importance to teachers. Unless they can identify and address the tacit understandings which provide the substance of those concepts, teachers cannot know what sense is being made of their efforts. This is not to argue that the development of second-order concepts is the real goal of history teaching, and substantive historical knowledge merely a vehicle. Assumptions of this kind account for the sterility of much recent public debate. The point of learning history is to understand the past, but if children are to achieve understanding their assumptions about what history is and how it works must be developed alongside it. Moreover, what children learn about the past in schools may be the end of their formal study of history, but is not necessarily the end of their acquisition of historical knowledge; the development of their second-order concepts may prove the limiting factor upon their future grasp of history.

Many children begin their study of history assuming that the past is somehow *given*, perhaps by direct inspection of pictures, films or videos; or they assume that history depends on a few surviving truthful statements by eyewitnesses. Where there were no truthful eyewitnesses, nothing can be said. For other pupils, statements about the past are information guaranteed by authority.[17] The shift from these understandings to a workable concept of evidence is a major one, and not all pupils will accomplish it by 16, but those who do achieve it begin to understand the basis of historical knowledge and one aspect of historians' agreements and disagreements. Those who remain in the position in which statements about the past are guaranteed by authority are vulnerable to violent swings to an opposite view, in which any version of the past is as good as any other, because historians all have their own reasons for saying what they say. The security of belief in the authoritative past is likely to give way in the face of its first encounters with historians' disagreements to a vicious relativism, and escape is sought by clinging for safety to a particular dogmatic historical creed or even a particular historian's work.

Similar sets of tacit understandings can be traced in connection with the development of other concepts, for example notions of *reasons* for action and *cause* in the area of explanation, of *change, continuity* and *significance* in the area of historical accounts and narrative. The willingness of pupils to write off historical agents as lacking any kind of rationality, and to treat past social practices as demonstrating that people in the past were seriously mentally defective, is now quite well documented, and there is a good deal of agreement about the way in which pupils' ideas develop in this area, at least up to the age of 16.[18]

Children's understanding of cause is perhaps more problematic, partly because the concept of cause is a contested one in philosophy, which makes it more difficult to agree about the analysis of children's ideas, and partly because there is less research evidence available.[19] The evidence of children's tacit understandings of change, continuity and significance suggests development from ideas of change as the discontinuous eruption of events, to working assumptions which include the idea that different rates of change may occur at the same time in different aspects of human affairs.[20] The actual relationship between pupils' understandings of change and significance, and their ideas about the differing bases of historians' accounts, is not yet clear. Work in this area is very limited, but it seems likely that pupils' assumptions about the construction and justification of historical accounts are at least as important as their ideas about evidence in determining their ability to cope with the openness of history without resorting to dogmatism or relativism, or collapsing into simple confusion.

Underlying pupils' thinking between 14 and 19 seems to be the idea of a past which *happens in stories*. Stories are *given* in the unfolding of events. (There is, of course, some reason for regarding patterns of action as internally related, and hence as unfolding, if incomplete, stories in the eyes of the agents involved.) But pupils' ideas seem to posit something complete and rigid, and to extend the conception to encompass events and processes. Where historians give different accounts, one or more of them is simply *wrong*. Disagreement must then be the result of incompetence, 'bias' (a notion which has probably done more damage in history teaching than any other) or of inadequate evidence. Incompetence is discovered by checking with the teacher which story the examiner is likely to want. 'Bias' is either simply 'detected' and ruled out (anything from basic methodological presuppositions to personal ambition can fall under this all-encompassing notion) or serves to show that history is merely subjective. Inadequate evidence is seen as a licence for, and possibly an explanation of, a generalized relativism. Once we understand more about this area of pupils' tacit understandings, it may be possible to teach with more assurance that pupils are learning what we hope they are learning, and that they understand what we assume they are understanding.

Structural generalizations
Pupils work with ideas about how and why things happen in the human past. Like the ideas which cluster around the structural concepts already discussed, these ideas would not necessarily be accepted by a professional historian. But because children have to employ *some* sets of ideas to make sense of what people did or suffered in the past, teachers have to consider and address such ideas, and try to improve their adequacy. This may mean teaching broad principles as heuristic devices, not as true statements about the past, still less as laws or lessons of history. Examples of generalizations of this kind include ideas such as that actions and policies can have unintended consequences; that what is 'normal' in human affairs is defined by reference to the past as well as to the present; that what can be made to happen is limited by what has happened as well as what (at any given moment) is happening; that the fact that some imagined possibilities have not been realized in the past does not mean that they are not feasible under new circumstances; and that beliefs and practices which seem to be illogical

and impractical are usually intelligible or rational within their own frames of reference.

It is easy to lampoon such statements as either half-baked or overblown. That, of course, is exactly what they are, and it is an important part of history teaching to encourage children to recognize this. But without such ideas as starting points, pupils will be left to struggle alone with the confusions of the past, and will work with other sets of generalizations which are likely to prove less appropriate and, in many cases, will simply impede the growth of understanding. Once again, if we are serious about history teaching in schools, we must recognize the need for serious research into the substance of pupils' ideas, the way those ideas relate to one another, and the effect of different learning and teaching approaches on their development.

Substantive generalizations

Besides the high-level structural generalizations already discussed, children operate with sets of substantive ideas or generalizations about key areas of human experience. These are not 'lessons of the past', but heuristic devices, starting points to be elaborated upon, modified, and if necessary discarded. They are not mechanically applicable: they require judgement and experience if they are not to mislead; but at the same time they help children develop that judgement and give shape to that experience. History is uniquely qualified to increase and enrich the stock of ideas which adolescents draw upon when thinking about both the past and the contemporary world: in that sense it offers vicarious experience. Examples of this kind of generalization might include the following: political power substantially depends upon the degree and quality of access to information, relative command of resources, and the perceived legitimacy of authority; wealth is not equivalent to money, although economies can work despite operating on this and other fallacious assumptions; the complexity of social systems is closely related to the size of disposable economic surpluses; political conscious-ness is shaped in part by a sense of history; this may apply to relations between peoples (eg the Irish and the British), or to the interpretation of events and actions (eg the Munich 'lesson' that dictators are not to be appeased, invoked in relations with Nasser and Galtieri).

The fact that statements of this kind are at best half-truths does not allow teachers to avoid them. History teachers must discover what sets of assumptions children are working with, assess their appropriateness, and develop new ones where necessary, while at the same time trying to reduce pupils' dependence on them. School history both extends the

repertoire of generalizations available to pupils, and demonstrates their
fallibility.

The importance of both structural and substantive generalizations is
very clear to anyone who has listened to pupils at work. The thirteen-
year-old children in the excerpt below are discussing the outbreak of the
Second World War, something which they have not studied at school.
What they *have* studied is the First World War. Nevertheless they have
both some particular information about the Second World War, and
sets of assumptions about how the world works and about appropriate
moves in historical explanation.

Andrea:	I think Hitler was a madman.
Stephanie:	He was . . . he was . . .
Andrea:	. . . and I think that's what, um . . .
Stephanie:	. . . a complete nutter . . .
Andrea:	. . .He wanted . . .
Stephanie:	He should have been put in a . . . er . . . um . . .
Andrea:	. . . a super-race . . .
Stephanie:	. . . thingy . . .
Andrea	. . . of blond, blue-eyed people . . .
Kirstin:	. . . um . . .
Stephanie:	Yeah – that followed him.
Andrea:	. . . to rule the world . . .
Stephanie:	Yeah – that followed him . . .
Andrea:	I mean, but he was a short, fat, dark-haired sort of person.
Kirstin:	Yeah.
Stephanie:	. . . little person.
Kirstin:	Could it be avoided? I don't think it could of.
Andrea:	No.
Kirstin:	If Hitler hadn't started . . . I mean I can't blame it on him, but if he hadn't started that and provoked . . . you know . . . us . . . if to say you know, that's wrong . . .
Stephanie:	It would have been . . .
Kirstin:	Yeah, it would have been, but it wasn't . . .
Stephanie:	Yeah, if you think about it, *every* war could've been avoided.
Andrea:	I reckon if Hitler hadn't come on the scene that would never have happened.
Kirstin:	Oh yeah, yes, yes . . .
Andrea:	There must've been other *underlying* things, like World War One we found out there was lots of underlying causes, not only . . .
Stephanie:	. . . um . . .
Andrea:	Franz Ferdinand being shot . . .

Stephanie:	Yeah ...
Kirstin:	... um ...
Andrea:	... but loads of other stuff as well.
Kirstin:	Oh yeah, I don't think he was so far ...
Andrea:	Yeah, there must've been a few other main currents ...
Kirstin:	But, like that Franz Ferdinand, he didn't get, that was the main starting point for it all, that really blew it up ...
Andrea:	But I don't know whether ... because we don't know any underlying causes ...
Kirstin:	... um ...
Stephanie:	Yeah, but most ...
Andrea:	... if Hitler *hadn't* been there, I don't know whether it could've been avoided or not.
Stephanie:	Yeah but most wars can be avoided anyway, I mean, if you think about it we could've avoided the First World War and *any* war ...
Kirstin:	... by discussing it.
Stephanie:	Exactly.
Kirstin:	Yeah you can avoid it, but I don't think ...
Andrea:	Yeah but not everybody's willing to discuss.
Stephanie:	Exactly, nobody just wants to sit down and do that, they just want to *do* something about it, so they start chucking bombs at each other.
Kirstin:	Yeah you could, but in another way you can't, can you, I mean it depends ...

The children here operate with second-order ideas about cause and explanation in history ('there must've been other *underlying* things . . .') which are likely to be helpful to them: they recognize that there may be important elements of an explanation that, in this case, they simply do not know. But they also work with substantive generalizations about the way wars may be started or avoided ('most wars can be avoided anyway' . . . 'by discussing it') which turn out to be highly misleading in the case of the Second World War. Second-order ideas and substantive generalizations have different values for different tasks: ignore either, and both teachers and children are likely to get into difficulty. Anyone trying to teach the Second World War to the pupils in this excerpt, without being aware of their ideas, is not likely to be very effective.

Substantive concepts
The problem of discovering the understandings with which pupils are operating is even more acute in the development of their substantive concepts. Pupils' notions of, for example, trade, king, tax, victory,

revolution, or power are based upon their own experiences both inside
and outside school: whatever pupils have encountered in school, much
of their understanding of the substantive concepts employed in history
will be shaped by experience outside it. Attempts to construct a single
'best' line of approach to understanding a notion like 'king' seem
doomed to failure because children approach such notions from many
different directions, and the 'best' one will be the one that builds on the
strengths of the particular ideas of individual pupils. The consequence
of all this is that teachers must have time to discover and develop the
existing understandings of their pupils. Since these understandings will
vary from pupil to pupil, they can seldom be predicted in advance. This
necessitates talk with pupils in an open framework which allows
children to develop their ideas and teachers to monitor them. The time
required will be considerable, and overloading the history curriculum is
likely to result in dire consequences of the kind familiar in *1066 and All
That*.

It is possible that the advent of the National Curriculum may enable
teachers to be more confident than hitherto that children will have
encountered certain concepts at particular stages of their schooling.
However, unless the history curriculum is laid down and monitored in
enormous detail there will be great variations in what is learned and
how it is taught, and the more fussy the specification, the more slippage
there will be in the practical processes of teaching. Draconian
specification will lead to absurdity, because the networks of ideas
available to children are so open and unpredictable; more acceptable
would be advisory guidance as to some of the major organizing
concepts in the key fields of human activity picked out for study. This
would be particularly appropriate if a workable solution could be found
to the problems of establishing a usable framework of British history.

A framework of knowledge

There is no disagreement that children need to know some history:
knowledge of the past is the point of the discipline. It is also widely
accepted that this means studying particular passages of history in
sufficient depth to make some sense of them. Although severe problems
arise when governments seek to determine in detail exactly *what* is to be
learnt, there is no reason to resist the claim that *part* of the historical
knowledge required by pupils should be a framework of British history
set in the wider context of European and world history. There is a great
difference between a government setting out broad guidelines, and
members of a government (who are neither teachers nor historians)

attempting to specify the details of a curriculum and what degree of detail there should be, particularly when the latter in practice determines *how* history is taught. The former is a sensible and legitimate part of establishing a national curriculum; the latter would be quite improper. There is little point here in discussing the improper course, if only because such a discussion would have to be, if it were not simply a waste of time, a piece of political persuasion. The idea of a framework, however, is a serious and legitimate challenge for those concerned with history teaching, and raises difficult questions, pointing up serious gaps in existing thinking.

A framework must meet the entirely sensible criteria of continuity and progression laid down by the government. It cannot meet these if it consists of a list of events, people and dates which are to be learned as discrete items of information and tested as such. In a spurious framework of this kind progression could be defined only in terms of accumulation: levels would be differentiated according to whether pupils knew one fact, ten facts or 20, and continuity could consist only in the maintenance of chronological order, whatever gaps and incoherence became apparent. How can a framework be constructed which avoids such absurdities, and yet does not fall into the trap of offering 'the story' of British history of the kind which would make it (in the Soviet sense) 'Party history'? Several criteria suggest themselves.

First, any framework must be an *overview*. In other words it must offer a coherent pattern, not a mere collection of facts and dates. Outlines which shed arbitrary pools of light in a sea of darkness have failed.

Second, a framework must be capable of *rapid* presentation: it should be a course that can be taught in two or three weeks, so that it does not degenerate into discrete factual outlines. If history teachers have learned anything in the past four decades it is that laying down facts gradually over the years in a slow chronological aggregation does not work. Unless pupils have some overall scheme into which to fit new knowledge, it cannot form part of a framework because there is no structure into which it can be fitted. Children simply forget most of what they learn in one year before they are half-way through the next. (A sedimentary model must give way to a metamorphic one.)

Third, a framework must be *thematic*. Initially it should be developmental, not one all-encompassing official *story*, because a developmental overview allows legitimate simplification, without handing on an interpretation as though it were on a par with discrete statements of fact. In their simplest form developmental frameworks

are concerned with change and continuity, with simplified long-term
patterns that are not, in the first instance, causal, and do not offer a
narrative in which actions are connected by reasons for doing things.
They fall some way short of full historical accounts, which are
organized in narrative form and are more or less explicitly explanatory.
Compared to developmental frameworks, these historical accounts are
highly complex. They simultaneously involve the intentions, purposes,
values, and beliefs of key figures, groups, and institutions, all referred
back to prior actions and policies of other agents, and to the purposes
and actions of other agents at the same time. They incorporate multiple
and complex causal relationships, links between every element of
human experience, and between those experiences and the natural
world, all traced backwards and forwards in time. They encompass an
indefinite number of simultaneous story-lines, each with its own
attributions of significance, all moving forward at once. We cannot
produce a simplified single version of this kind of story to serve as a
framework of British history which is not either Party history or
absurdly too complicated for young children. A thematic and developmental framework avoids this dilemma.

Fourth, a framework must be a *progressive structure* which can
gradually be elaborated and differentiated, gaining in thematic coherence through internal links, both causal and intentional. It must link an
increasing range of themes, and allow gradual geographical extension.

Fifth, a framework must be an *open structure*, capable of being tested,
modified, abandoned or improved. It must allow students to fit new
material into it without modification or, where appropriate, to change
the structure to accommodate new learning and new perspectives.

Finally a framework must be a *usable structure* offering perspectives
which enable pupils to cope with new encounters with the past, and to
handle the present and the future. History is only valuable when it is not
inert: when it changes the way we can see things.

The kind of framework suggested here depends on the notion of a
developmental and thematic overview which is slowly elaborated and
'thickened' into full historical accounts as pupils move through school.
Such a framework allows simplification in a legitimate way: themes can
be articulated into a small number of parts, and from early on several
strands are possible, not 'the' single version. It allows pupils to make
their own assessments of the significance of changes or putative changes
on the basis of initially simple but gradually more complex criteria.
Who or what was affected? How many? In what way? How long for? As
the structure grows more complex it allows new criteria to be learnt and

increasing internal connection to be made within and between themes, so that they may progressively approach the status of accounts, but with no pretence to be 'the' story. It encourages pupils to see that the content of a framework changes with the questions it is accommodating. It enables teachers to return constantly to the framework to slot in new material, or to use new material to encourage children to test the structure. In addition such a framework has two very practical benefits: it allows considerable freedom for the rest of the history timetable, and it obviates the need to divide content in a mechanical way between primary and secondary schooling.

The most significant question about a framework, however, is whether it can be tested as a *framework* rather than as a collection of the individual facts from which it is constituted. There is no existing system which can be borrowed for this purpose, but recent developments in assessment suggest a possible approach.[21] This involves testing a framework against a set of criteria, which might include some or all of the following:

> *Coherence:* the ability to make increasingly complex internal connections, and to shift to a more explanatory structure.
> *Mobility:* the ability to move up and down the temporal scale and across a spatial range, making long-term links or comparisons, and changing attributions of significance as the scale is changed.
> *Dimensionality:* the ability to pick out relationships and make connections between strands; the identification of disparate changes and parallel developments.
> *Resolution:* the ability to expand sections of the framework to show how the overall picture stands up to detailed study.
> *Revisability:* the ability, when faced with new material which does not easily fit the framework, to locate the pinch points and to change the structure or alter assessments of importance to allow a better fit.
> *Field:* the ability to incorporate wider areas and longer time-spans.
> *Applicability:* the ability to integrate new material or to shed light on periods not yet investigated, or on the present.

Assessment of pupils' knowledge on the basis of criteria of this kind would allow candidates to use whatever knowledge they had acquired during any key stage. It would not force pupils to commit to short-term memory large quantities of discrete pieces of information, but it would demand that they could operate with a framework which could organize and make sense of British history in an appropriate way. The knowledge required would be ordered knowledge but not a single story, and the components of the framework would be fixed only in the sense that they would constitute an historically defensible and accurate version of British history.

Conclusion

History means learning about the past. Of course the past must be simplified. Of course children will need some stories to make sense of it. What they do *not* need is *the* story of the whole British past: they need a workable framework. However even the best framework is only part of a history curriculum, and pupils need to learn more about history than that. A proper framework creates room for manoeuvre in a sensible history curriculum.

Pupils need time to examine passages of the past in detail. But they need to learn more about history than what happened in the past; they need some understanding of the discipline itself. And for this, too, time is a critical requirement. Children need time to talk. Teachers need time to listen. Moreover, if history really *is* important, then we all need to know more about how children learn it and about the tacit understandings which play such a central role in their learning. This means there must be time for reflection and research, not necessarily by people in so-called ivory towers, but by teams of teachers too. And that means more time. An overloaded, overspecified history curriculum taught by overstretched teachers is a recipe for disaster. It is not difficult to avoid most of the problems of overloading which could cause such a disaster: all that is required is some attention to professional rather than political criteria for the construction of a curriculum. Serious commitment to understanding better how children learn history has tougher consequences in terms of the costs involved in giving real opportunities to teachers, and resourcing research and curriculum development. But then in recent years we have become accustomed to hearing that tough decisions must be faced. The touchstone of a society's (or a politician's) serious intent in educating its children in history, as in everything else, is whether society is prepared to pay the price.

A national curriculum with a firm place for history for all pupils is a highly desirable change of direction for education in Britain. A coherent history curriculum for pupils between the ages of five and 16, offering continuity and progression, and the opportunity to monitor both, would be a major step forward. It would be tragic if these prospects were to turn sour because the interests of serious history teaching and the knowledge and experience of professional teachers were overridden by the political or social goals of small groups of politically motivated men and women who have given nothing to history teaching in the past. History in schools is too important to be left to the politicians.

Notes

1. Oakeshott, M. (1962), 'The activity of being an historian'. In: M. Oakeshott, *Rationalism in Politics*. London: Methuen (pp. 137–167).
2. See the remark of N. Khrushchev, quoted in DES (1985), *History in the Primary and Secondary Years: An HMI View*. London: HMSO (p. 1).
3. Lee, P.J. (1984), 'Why learn history'. In: A.K. Dickinson, P.J. Lee, and P.J. Rogers (eds), *Learning History*. London: Heinemann Educational Books (pp. 1–19).
4. Kitson Clark, G. (1967), *The Critical Historian*. London: Heinemann Educational Books (pp. 4–9, pp. 48–9).
5. Ibid., p. 7.
6. DES and the Welsh Office (1990), *National Curriculum History Working Group: Final Report*. London: DES.
7. For discussion of the central relationships here see Danto, A.C. (1965), *Analytical Philosophy of History*. Cambridge: Cambridge University Press. A more recent contribution from a very different point of view is to be found in White, H. (1987), 'The value of narrativity in the representation of reality'. In H. White, *The Content of the Form*. Baltimore: Johns Hopkins University Press (pp. 1–25).
8. Much of the recent discussion in the press muddles social and historical criteria. See, for example, Skidelsky, R. (1989), 'Battle of Britain's past times'. *Independent*, 22 August 1989.
9. Keatinge, M.W., (1910), *Studies in the Teaching of History*. London: Black.
10. Skidelsky, R. op. cit.
11. The most curious feature of the Report is its concept of 'essential information' in the History Study Units. *Information* is presumably something short of *knowledge*; it is accepted in good faith without the recipient necessarily having a proper understanding of the grounds on which it might rest (which is why we can talk of people being misinformed, and even of disinformation). This moves away from the emphasis on knowledge as something understood in relation to evidence that seems central to other parts of the Report. The idea that some information is essential presumably implies that information not so characterized is inessential. (The alternative is that the Report is indulging in vacuous contrast, or, worse, pulling a cheap trick: 'There is more essential information, but we won't tell you what it is!') The difficulty is that what is listed is not actually information, but subheadings for topics, and that much of it could only somewhat idiosyncratically be regarded as essential in any valid sense, particularly if we are not informed as to what questions are to be asked. This area of the Report more than any other betrays the political pressures under which the History Working Group was operating;

not through crude interference with its deliberations, but through the more subtle pressure of public pronouncements at the outset, and again in reaction to the Interim Report. It remains to be seen how far the National Curriculum Council will respond to this sort of pressure.

12. Work on pupils' tacit understandings is still in its infancy; more has been carried out or is in process than has been published. None of it is more than suggestive, most of it is flawed, but this does not mean that it can be ignored. The following exemplify some of the main stages in the development of research:

Thompson, D. (1972), 'Some psychological aspects of history teaching'. In: W.H. Burston and C.W. Green (eds), *Handbook for History Teachers*. London: Methuen Educational (pp. 18–38). (This is a useful summary of work up to the early 1970s.); Hallam, R.N. (1966), 'An investigation into some aspects of the historical thinking of children and adolescents.' Leeds: MEd. thesis, University of Leeds; Hallam, R.N. (1975), 'A study of the effect of teaching method on the growth of logical thought with special reference to the teaching of history.' Leeds: PhD. thesis, University of Leeds; Rees, A. (1976), 'Teaching strategies for the assessment and development of thinking skills in history.' London: MPhil. thesis, University of London; Dickinson, A.K. and Lee, P.J. (1978), 'Understanding and research'. In: A.K. Dickinson and P.J. Lee (eds), *History Teaching and Historical Understanding*. London: Heinemann Educational Books (pp. 94–120); Shemilt, D. (1983), 'The devil's locomotive', *History and Theory*, 22, 1–18; Booth, M.B. (1983), 'Skills, concepts and attitudes: the development of adolescent children's historical thinking', *History and Theory*, 22, 101–117; Shemilt, D. (1984), 'Beauty and the philosopher: empathy in history and the classroom'. In: A.K. Dickinson, P.J. Lee, and P.J. Rogers, (eds), *Learning History*, op. cit. (pp. 39–84); Shemilt, D. (1987), 'Adolescent ideas about evidence and methodology in history'. In: C. Portal (ed.), *The History Curriculum for Teachers*. Lewes: The Falmer Press (pp. 39–61); Ashby, R. and Lee, P.J. (1987), 'Children's concepts of empathy and understanding in history'. In: C. Portal (ed.), op. cit. (pp. 62–88).

In addition to the research listed here there is the work carried out by the Southern Regional Examinations Board (SREB) in examining SCHP 13–16, which allowed it to acquire a considerable quantity of data and a great deal of expertise. While there are significant differences in the conceptual and empirical assumptions of the research, all the work cited supports the proposition that children's ideas are of central importance. Research in other disciplines suggests the same conclusion.

13. The efforts of the History Working Group to produce a report which would receive support from all quarters demonstrates the problems. Discussion of the Interim Report at a colloquium at Chatham House (5

September 1989) showed how any attempt at a single account is in practice likely to get short shrift from historians.

14. G. Stedman Jones argued at a conference at Ruskin College, Oxford (3 June 1989) that pupils must have some sort of story before they can deconstruct one. There is some truth in this, but logical presupposition does not necessitate temporal priority. Pupils must have *some* stories, but these will be components of an overall account, not an overall account itself, and it is the latter which raises the problems.

15. See the works cited in the list above, including the work of the SREB.

16. The discussion which follows owes so much to discussions with Denis Shemilt that it is hard to say which parts of it are mine and which his. The responsibility for any absurdities which may have crept in is of course entirely mine.

17. Shemilt, D. (1987), 'Adolescent ideas about evidence and methodology in history'. op. cit. (pp. 39–61); Ashby, R. and Lee P.J. (1987), 'Discussing the evidence'. *Teaching History*, 48, (pp. 13–17).

18. Lee, P.J. (1978), 'Explanation and understanding in history'. In: A.K. Dickinson and P.J. Lee (eds), op. cit. (pp. 72–93); Dickinson, A.K. and Lee, P.J. (1978), 'Understanding and research'. In: A.K. Dickinson and P.J. Lee (eds), op. cit. (pp. 94–120); Shemilt, D. (1984), 'Beauty and the philosopher: empathy in history and the classroom'. In: A.K. Dickinson, P.J. Lee, and P.J. Rogers, (eds), op. cit. (pp. 39–84); Dickinson, A.K. and Lee, P.J. (1984), 'Making sense of history'. In: A.K. Dickinson, P.J. Lee, and P.J. Rogers, (eds), op. cit. (pp. 117–153); Booth, M.B. *et al.* (1986), *Empathy in History: from definition to assessment.* Eastleigh: Southern Regional Examinations Board; Ashby, R. and Lee, P.J. (1987), 'Children's concepts of empathy and understanding in history'. In: C. Portal (ed.), op. cit. (pp. 62–88).

The Booth et. al. pamphlet puts too much emphasis on a relatively mechanical criterion, 'differentiated historical empathy', as opposed to the ability to 'cash in' what is understood in order to explain some aspect of social behaviour or individual action.

19. Shemilt, D. (1983), 'The devil's locomotive'. *History and Theory*, 22, 1–18. Should pupils who seem to be working with a non-Humean conception of causes as 'powerful particulars' be classified as at a lower level than those who seem to recognize that attributions of cause imply some sort of generalization, however qualified?

20. Shemilt, D. (1980), *Evaluation Study.* Edinburgh: Holmes MacDougall; Sansom, C.J. (1987), 'Concepts, skills and content: a developmental approach to the history syllabus'. In: C. Portal (ed.), op. cit. (pp. 116–141).

21. The criteria suggested in what follows owe a great deal to the ideas of Denis Shemilt and John Hamer. The changes made to those ideas in this paper are largely marginal.

Chapter Four
Assessing, Recording and Reporting Children's Achievements: from Changes to Genuine Gains

Alaric Dickinson

Introduction

Assessment is a key element in educational practice. In its many forms it is an integral part of the process of teaching and learning, essential for monitoring standards and a powerful instrument of change. Sound formative assessment, for instance, is a necessary condition of good classroom practice and needs to be present in some form in every lesson. Used sensitively and perceptively, formative assessment can provide rich evidence of the achievements and learning difficulties of each pupil, and useful insights into what is needed next in terms of teaching and resources. Many teachers have also found it to be a particularly constructive and satisfying, though very time-consuming part of their work. This view is echoed here by a student teacher reflecting, in his log, on his teaching practice experience:

> Responding to children's work and ideas is one of the most interesting and rewarding aspects of my teaching practice. It is through this that I can engage with each pupil, see where he or she is at, and give my personal advice and words of praise, encouragement or constructive criticism. Alexis, for instance, was disruptive at first. His homework was sloppy and poor. Eventually my comments and constructive criticism helped to bring about major changes. The improvement was really moving. Unfortunately the time I have to work with each child isn't enough to go deeply into their work. But the potential to establish a positive relationship and motivate pupils through responding to their work and ideas is definitely one of the important lessons I have learned during teaching practice.[1]

Summative assessment is also a powerful instrument for change and one which can be used by people who seldom, if ever, enter classrooms. In the late 1980s widespread concern about standards of teaching and learning led to the advocacy of more formal assessment in many countries, not least in England and Wales where the 1988 Education Reform Act (ERA) imposed a national assessment system. This system requires that pupils' performance be assessed in relation to attainment targets by a combination of national external tests and assessment by teachers, and be reported on at ages 7,11,14 and 16.[2]

Past experience provides evidence that major assessment initiatives can have significant repercussions which may be intended or unexpected, beneficial or negative. Professor Ted Wragg, after studying some of the changes in pupil assessment made in the United States in the 1980s, has sounded a number of warnings about the mass testing developed in many American schools.[3] Underpinning these initiatives was a conviction that standards should be raised and that this could be achieved by applying the methods of business to education; in particular, setting discrete objectives, regular testing of children to measure whether the objectives were being achieved, and the use of test scores as performance indicators in the same way that profit levels might be regarded as evidence of success in business. Professor Wragg reported that these ideas led to such a volume and frequency of testing in some schools in North America that the use of optical scanning equipment to read and score test papers was the only feasible way of coping. In his experience teachers spent so much time on creating detailed records that they rarely consulted them, initiatives were judged almost entirely by their effects on test scores, and education was increasingly evaluated on the basis of easily scored and profiled tests which required little more than recall, recognition or low levels of understanding.[4]

National testing and assessment initiatives such as the ERA proposals for England and Wales will not necessarily lead to the problems highlighted by Professor Wragg, but his comments help to substantiate the case for thorough consideration and monitoring of major assessment initiatives. Decisions about national testing and assessment are certain to have a significant influence on the nature and future of history in education in the country concerned, and decisions about record keeping and reporting of children's achievements are also likely to have important ramifications. Assessment, recording and reporting arrangements should, therefore, be very carefully scrutinized, monitored and revised as appropriate. It is important to establish, for instance, which approaches to history are encouraged – and discouraged – by the imposed assessment arrangements, the effect of the new assessment arrangements upon the kind of formative assessment highlighted in the extract above, how far they enrich or disrupt learning and the extent to which the statutory assessment and reporting will prove beneficial to all concerned. The aims of this chapter are to explore, with particular reference to history, the national testing and assessment arrangements created under the ERA and, in so doing, to draw attention to some important questions, issues and criteria in pursuit of real gains for pupils, teachers and the wider community.

The ERA: beginnings of a great experiment

What assessment arrangements have been stipulated?
Section 2 of the ERA stipulates that the curriculum for every maintained school shall specify for each foundation subject:

(a) the knowledge, skills and understanding which pupils of different abilities and maturities are expected to have at the end of each key stage [referred to as 'attainment targets'];
(b) the matters, skills and processes which are required to be taught to pupils of different abilities and maturities during each key stage [referred to as 'programmes of study']; and
(c) the arrangements for assessing pupils at or near the end of each key stage for the purposes of ascertaining what they have achieved in relation to the attainment targets for that stage [referred to as 'assessment arrangements'].[5]

The Act further states (Section 4) that the Secretary of State may by Order specify, amend and update these three interdependent but separable components of the National Curriculum. Assessment, record-keeping and reporting are also carefully distinguished in the Act, and Section 218.1 states that:

[The Secretary of State may by regulations make provision] with respect to the keeping, disclosure and transfer of educational records about pupils at schools and such institutions and the supply of copies of such records to such persons, and in such circumstances as may be determined by or under the regulations.

Thus, for England and Wales, the Secretary of State can prescribe for record-keeping and reporting as well as attainment targets, programmes of study and assessment arrangements. Non-statutory guidance on implementation of the National Curriculum and assessment arrangements is provided by the National Curriculum Council (NCC) and the School Examinations and Assessment Council (SEAC) respectively.

The attainment targets are the pivotal component. Given their pre-eminence and the desire to implement the new scheme with haste, tensions have arisen between attainment targets and assessment arrangements. This was first evident in relation to mathematics and science. The report of the Task Group on Assessment and Testing (TGAT Report)[6] was published half-way through the deliberations of the National Curriculum Working Groups for science and mathematics, and the final reports for these two subjects were completed before the Secretary of State informed Parliament (on 7 June 1988) of the framework for assessment that the Government had decided to prescribe in the light of consultations and responses to TGAT's recommendations. One consequence of such piecemeal development of the curriculum and assessment arrangements has been considerable variation in the number of attainment targets prescribed. At the time of writing (August 1990) there are 17 attainment targets for science, 14 for mathematics, seven for geography, three for history and just one for technology.

The main principles which were to form the basis for a national system of assessment and testing in England and Wales were set out in the Secretary of State's announcement of 7 June 1988 as follows:

(a) attainment targets will be set which establish what children should normally be expected to know, understand and be able to do at the ages of 7, 11, 14 and 16; these will enable the progress of each child to be measured against national standards;

(b) pupils' performance in relation to attainment targets should be assessed and reported on at ages 7, 11, 14 and 16. Attainment targets should be grouped for this purpose to make the assessment and reporting manageable;

(c) different levels of attainment and overall pupil progress demonstrated by tests and assessment should be registered on a 10-point scale covering all the years of compulsory schooling;

(d) assessment should be by a combination of national external tests and assessment by teachers. At age 16 the GCSE will be the main form of assessment, especially in the core subjects of English, mathematics and science;

(e) the results of tests and other assessments should be used both formatively to help better teaching and to inform decisions about the next steps for a pupil, and summatively at ages 7, 11, 14 and 16 to inform parents about their child's progress;

(f) detailed results of assessment of individual pupils should be given in full to parents, and the Government attaches great importance to the principle that these reports should be simple and clear. Individuals' results should not be published, but aggregated results at the ages of 11, 14 and 16 should be so that the wider public can make informed judgements about attainment in a school and LEA. There should be no legal requirement for schools to publish results for 7 year olds, though it is strongly recommended that schools should do so;

(g) in order to safeguard standards, assessments made by teachers should be compared with the results of the national tests and with the judgements of other teachers.[7]

The wording of this announcement indicated that the government had broadly accepted the recommendations of TGAT. Under the new scheme pupils' levels of attainment were to be assessed at or near the end of each key stage by a combination of national external tests and moderated teacher assessments in relation to attainment targets and statements of attainment. This also meant that ten levels of attainment had to be established for each attainment target plus a statement of attainment for each level. These statements of attainment (descriptions of what pupils must know, understand and be able to do in order to show that they have attained a particular level) were to be part of the Statutory Orders.

The wording of the Act indicates that details of the assessment, recording and reporting arrangements will be worked out over several years and that SEAC will advise the Secretary of State and, 'if so requested by him, assist him to carry out programmes of research and development'.[8] Given the radical changes initiated by the ERA it was inevitable that a variety of problems would occur and that SEAC and the NCC would be called upon to offer advice on a great many issues. Sometimes the advice has been accepted, sometimes not. On reporting, for instance, the government decided that schools should provide parents with an annual report on their children's progress, although SEAC had advised that the statutory requirement should be a record of achievement including assessment reports sent to parents at the end of each key stage.

A much more serious issue has been the nature and role of the national tests. TGAT suggested that a wide range of Standard Assessment Tasks (SATs) should be at the heart of the national assessment system, that these SATs should involve practical, oral and written tasks done in such a way that pupils would not see them as being any different from normal classroom work, and that teachers' ratings of pupil performance should be used as a fundamental element of the national assessment system. The first trials of SATs for pupils at the end of the first key stage (KS1) in the core subjects of English, science and mathematics in summer 1990 confirmed fears that such tests would seriously reduce teaching time and over-burden both pupils and teachers. In the light of these trials SEAC recommended that the time spent administering SATs to pupils aged seven should be limited to 50 per cent of teaching time over three weeks. One implication of such a limitation is that SATs at KS1 are likely to cover only a sample of the attainment targets in the core subjects (though teacher assessment will cover all aspects of both core and foundation subjects). This in turn raises questions not only about sampling arrangements but also about the nature and main purpose of SATs. For instance, if SATs are intended to provide national (and local) information on general standards and on changes in standards over time, and to help guide and check teachers' assessments in relation to all attainment targets, then there is a strong case for sample testing of all attainment targets. Logically children would be selected into sample groups and tested on different attainment targets. If, on the other hand, SATs exist primarily to check teachers' assessments on particular aspects of the curriculum and to provide standardized information for parents then all children should be tested on the same (restricted) range of attainment targets. At first sight this particular issue appears to be a problem for science and mathematics rather than for history which has a much smaller number of attainment targets. In fact, both this and various other issues arising from the national assessment scheme could have profound consequences for the teaching and learning of history in the school years.

Assessment arrangements for history
When the Secretary of State created the History Working Group in January 1989 his terms of reference directed the members to take account of the framework for assessment and testing that he had announced on 7 June 1988. He also said: 'In particular the Working Group should offer advice in broad terms about assessment and testing in relation to the attainment targets recommended, the grouping of those targets for purposes of reporting the results of assessment, and in particular what might appropriately be measured by nationally prescribed tests.'[9] It should be noted that the Group was to offer only broad advice on assessment and testing. The earlier decision about

statements of attainment meant that this, and the other Working Groups established after June 1988, were required to produce ten levels of attainment plus a statement of attainment for each attainment target. This formula had been established before the groups began their deliberations. It remained to be seen whether progressive advances in what it was thought children should know, understand and be able to do in terms of each attainment target could be not only stated with the necessary clarity and precision but also, and very important, measured by means of tests and valid and reliable teacher assessments. Such tests and assessments would also have to be sensitive and simple enough to enable the (rapid) detection, by examiners and teachers, of the ten levels for each attainment target.

The issue which immediately proved very controversial was the assessment of historical knowledge. The History Working Group's proposals included the assertion that, in their view, 'the best, and indeed the only, practical way to ensure that historical knowledge as information is taught, learned, and assessed is by clearly spelling out the essential historical information in the programmes of study and assessing it through the attainment targets'.[10] A particularly thought-provoking critique of their proposals was issued by the History Curriculum Association (HCA) which asserted that a skills-based assessment model had been imposed on a knowledge-based subject.[11] Suggestions by this and other pressure groups ranged from the idea that the only way to discover how much pupils have learned about a topic is to test them for their knowledge of it, to views that the amount of knowledge and the ability to use it should enter into the judgement of how successfully a task has been completed, and that testing for knowledge should be testing for pupils' ability to transform facts into understanding. Other ideas put forward included the proposal that knowledge should be tested in a way which enables pupils to select information appropriate to the task, and that a balance should be secured between knowledge which pupils themselves bring to their tasks and knowledge which will be provided in the questions.

Meanwhile the Secretary of State, upon receiving the Final Report in April 1990, asked SEAC to advise him 'whether assessment against the attainment targets, as recommended in the report, will reliably reflect a pupil's level of knowledge within each study unit'. After receiving their reply he announced that he had decided to accept two of the attainment targets recommended by the Group (AT2 and AT3), to propose that AT1 should be called 'knowledge and understanding of history', and also to propose that 'the fourth attainment target should be reexamined with a view to combining its constituent statements of attainment with those under the other three attainment targets'.[12] The problem of appropriate weighting for AT1, and of revising the statements of attainment, was passed temporarily to the NCC, with his comment that he attached special importance to assessment against AT1 because it could measure more directly what pupils have learned from their historical studies, that he thought his proposed AT1 should carry a higher weighting than the other targets for the purposes of assessment, and that he sought their advice on this matter.

For over a year the controversy concerning testing directly for knowledge deflected public attention away from several other problems emanating from the statutory assessment requirements. These required that levels of attainment and overall pupil progress, in relation to prescribed attainment targets, must be demonstrated by tests and teacher assessment and registered on a ten point scale. These requirements were based on the TGAT report and critics increasingly referred to them as the TGAT model. In fairness to the authors, it should be stressed that their document was a detailed one with 227 paragraphs, 14 appendices and 44 recommendations in the main report alone! Critics of the TGAT model apropos history have asserted that it seems inappropriate for assessing some attainments (in particular testing directly for knowledge); that history is not amenable to the neat, progressive and formative model advocated by TGAT; and that the History Working Group did not apply the model properly. In their Final Report the History Working Group did in fact express some doubts about the model (see, for instance, p. 119). Other critics, notably the HCA, have asserted that criterion-referencing, with its demand that tasks be specified separately and tested discretely, cuts across the holistic nature of historical learning. Clearly it is necessary to consider seriously whether the arrangements are appropriate for assessing and testing history. Are parts of the model inappropriate for history? Can the problems be overcome? If not, what changes are appropriate for the assessment of school history?

In a recent discussion paper on the TGAT model Dr Tim Lomas suggested that the two main difficulties for history are the need to dismember what some consider a holistic area into coherent elements as identified in separate attainment targets, and the requirement for a linear model of ten progressively more demanding levels.[13] The model proposed by TGAT defines levels arbitrarily by the attainment of median students in an age cohort. Among the problems of using such a linear model for history Dr Lomas lists the complexity of pupils' progress, the fact that progress cannot be described in simple statements, and that external factors affect pupils' progression in history. The authors of the TGAT Report have also been criticized for expecting that a subject-free model could be applied across all curriculum areas, but it should be stressed that their report includes the proposal that 'exceptions from one or more of its requirements be allowed if substantial reasons for the exceptions can be provided'.[14] They also acknowledge concern about the practicability of identifying and assessing separate components in subjects where pupils' work is holistic in nature (for example, art and music) but express confidence that 'it is possible to devise tasks of a holistic kind which still allow the identification of separate elements for assessment purposes without jeopardising the coherence of the whole'.[15]

Undoubtedly there are problems inherent in the assessment arrangements proposed so far, some of which may be solved more easily than others. For instance, there are practical problems such as the need for all concerned to understand and employ effectively ten statements of attainment per attainment target. A more permanent problem is the lack of research on progression which has led inevitably to much 'rough speculation'. Further problems arise from the fact that existing research, though limited, suggests that progression in history is affected by many variables and does not advance smoothly through a series of distinct stages.

Another major problem is the lack of an alternative model capable of solving the problems that have been identified by critics of the TGAT model! While this situation prevails, it seems appropriate to make the best use that is possible of the chosen model. In support of the TGAT model one can say that the statements of attainment for history are far fewer in number than those for science and mathematics and geography; that history examiners and teachers have been foremost among the pioneers of differentiation by outcome and levels-of-response assessment; and that history can benefit from not insignificant research on the development of pupils' understanding and ideation. Consequently statements of attainment for history seem less likely to need the kind of modification required in some subjects, for instance science and mathematics. In addition, studies in history combining analysis of the nature of history, innovative assessment techniques and careful empirical investigation have shown that it is possible to achieve clear distinctions between each of four or five levels.[16] This, and TGAT's acknowledgement that some special arrangements may be appropriate, provide further grounds for hope.

An effective national assessment scheme for history needs wide agreement on the characteristics of good school history and on appropriate levels of attainment. Recent debates about attainment targets and assessment of knowledge and understanding may prove to be a positive influence. Further consultation, research and classroom experience should certainly enable more precise statements of attainment to be formulated. It may also be possible to devise assessment tasks which circumvent the problems arising from the TGAT model. But how likely is it that the testing and assessment arrangements arising from the ERA will, in the 1990s, lead to real gains in the teaching and learning of history?

Initial optimism, caution and concern
At the beginning of a great 'natural experiment' created by imposed policy changes there are firm grounds for believing that standards in history and elsewhere can be raised by the kind of assessment arrangements initiated by the ERA. There is considerable evidence that history in schools in England and Wales prior to the 1988 Act was good in parts but bad or non-existent in others. Primary school history seems to have been the greatest problem. The National Monitoring System 1982-86 reported that standards in history were adjudged by Her Majesty's Inspectors to be satisfactory or better in only one in five infant schools and one in three junior schools.[17] Three years later HM Senior Chief Inspector of Schools said in his annual report, 'history and geography hardly exist in practice in many primary schools'.[18]
Attainment targets, programmes of study, tests and teacher assessment seem likely to focus the attention of teachers and learners more consistently than hitherto on the objectives underpinning schemes of work. Pupils should benefit from clear targets established by the statutory reporting (provided this is supplemented by teachers' regular assessments and informal comments). The information parents will receive concerning their children's progress in relation to the prescribed attainment targets should draw parents further into what is being attempted. Governing bodies, LEAs and the wider community will have more data about the achievements of each school, and the comparative aggregated information about pupils' achievements can be used, in the words of a DES publication on the National Curriculum, 'as an indicator of where there needs to be further effort, resources, changes in the curriculum, etc'.[19] It is also encouraging that both the ERA and subsequent non-statutory statements have acknowledged the need to review and update the assessment and reporting arrangements.

The responsibility of the Secretary of State for Education to revise the National Curriculum when necessary and desirable is built into the legislation, the NCC and SEAC have been created to advise him and to keep all aspects of the curriculum and assessment arrangements under review, and the DES has stated in print that 'the experiences of teachers and their professional advice will give essential indications, right from the outset, of the need for and nature of changes'.[20] All this encourages optimism.

However, there are also some grounds for caution and concern. For instance, the additional demands on teachers' time must be taken very seriously. It is vital that teachers' commitment to extensive formative assessment is sustained following the introduction of statutory testing and reporting. Losses would heavily outweigh gains if the introduction of statutory summative assessment towards the end of each key stage was accompanied by the demise of much of the formative assessment traditionally seen as part of the work and duty of a teacher. To what extent, one wonders, will the new arrangements advance or impede thorough and frequent formative assessment?

Much also depends on how open-minded and willing key decision-makers are to make a serious effort to understand the professional advice they receive. When central government controls so many aspects of education it is very important that major decisions are based on the best possible reasoning and understanding of the issues involved. On many matters so far the government has not only consulted but also acted upon the advice it has received. There are indications, however, of some key decisions being made in line with political convictions, rather than on advice arising from the consultative machinery created by the government.[21]

It is also possible that the level of prescription by central government may prove counter-productive. In this context the letter of 10 August 1989 from the Secretary of State to the chairman of the History Working Group, acknowledging receipt of the Interim Report, is of considerable interest. The following extract indicates the government's readiness to prescribe in detail what should be taught and assessed in schools:

> The group will in any case need to prepare detailed programmes of study for all the history study units, spelling out the additional or more advanced content of knowledge – including dates, events and people – that must be taught to pupils working towards each successive level of attainment . . . Other matters which I should be glad if the Group could

examine further include ... the detailed assessment issues listed in paragraph 6.9 of the interim report – in particular, how pupils' display of factual knowledge should be treated for assessment purposes.[22]

This intervention, his subsequent decision that there should be a special period of consultation prior to the statutory consultation led by the NCC, and his proposal for three attainment targets rather than the four (initially five) recommended by the History Working Group, all provide evidence of the extent of political control now being exercised over the curriculum in England and Wales. These actions also suggest that the advice of a working group (which was vetted and appointed by the government) and the wishes expressed by most teachers who participated in the consultation process may simply be ignored when a key decision is taken. Of course, the Secretary of State was acting within his statutory powers. What is certain is that the decisions finally taken on the matters raised by him will have profound effects on the future of history in education in England and Wales, and on the morale of teachers.

The decision of the Secretary of State (July 1990) to recommend a reduction in the compulsory requirements within the programmes of study recommended in the Final Report, and the History Working Group's own recommendation of 'a further set of themes to be designed by the schools themselves, drawing on their particular expertise and on local history, within specified ground rules'[23] are both welcome, because the more that content is prescribed the more the professionalism of teachers is undermined. However, more choice regarding content can create assessment problems, particularly in respect of claims to reliability. Johnson-Laird and Wason have shown that performance can be dramatically improved on tasks if they are related more closely to the subjects' experience.[24] Difficulty, it seems, is not so much intrinsic to the logical structure of a task but to its content and mode of presentation.

Research and classroom experience also suggest that gender differences can be an important factor. For example, Dickinson and Lee found in a pencil and paper test based on an aspect of naval warfare that five of the six pupils in a class of 30 who 'achieved' category one responses (the lowest level) were girls.[25] All these girls, when answering a questionnaire before the test, said that they had not read or seen a film or TV programme or done anything for themselves outside school concerning the First World War. In contrast, twelve boys in the same class had done something on the war, including six on naval aspects, two on the battle of Jutland and one on the actual naval manoeuvre (the focal point of the sources used in the test). Unfortunately this particular study did not explore gender effects further but there is considerable evidence, from research and examinations, that children's performance varies considerably from test to test (and within tests). Clearly this has important implications for national testing, teacher assessment and reporting. These implications include, for instance, a need for caution in drawing conclusions based on scores achieved in a single test at a particular time and in a particular situation.

There is also a need to bear in mind that decisions may have totally unintended and unwelcome consequences. For instance, one consequence of the legislation introduced in the mid-1980s to ensure that teachers worked 1,265 hours per year has been the demise in a great many schools of all extra-curricular activities! Such happenings emphasize the importance of examining all reforms in education very thoroughly prior to implementation, and monitoring them carefully in practice. The importance of careful scrutiny and well-informed arguments has been reinforced, in England and Wales, by the government's encouragement of consultation and the fact that the ERA empowers the Secretary of State for Education to specify, amend and update the National Curriculum. Many features of the national assessment arrangements merit extensive consideration and evaluation not only because of their potential influence as powerful agents of change but also because they are largely untried. For all subjects, designing and using valid criterion-referenced assessments on the scale proposed is a new venture which may prove very problematic and will certainly require considerable training of teachers. For history, the ten statements of attainment for each attainment target are a major concern because they constitute a new and radical development, based on little evidence but with profound implications for teaching and assessment. In history there are also the problems of how children's grasp of factual knowledge and understanding, explanation and interpretation, and their ability to evaluate historical information can be assessed satisfactorily. It will be important to take recent research and examination experience into account to avoid mistaken assumptions as to what pupils can and cannot do.

This brief tour of the ERA assessment arrangements and beginnings of a great national experiment has indicated a number of issues and questions, some of general interest and some specific to history. Questions of general interest include 'What are the likely implications for teaching and learning of the new assessment arrangements and programmes of study?'; 'Will teachers have time to carry out the assessment and recording arrangements satisfactorily?'; 'What will be the mechanism and timetable for revising the arrangements?'; and 'Will the arrangements be so prescriptive as to undermine seriously the professionalism of teachers?' Subject specific concerns include 'What kind of history will be encouraged by the assessment arrangements?'; 'Are the attainment targets and statements of attainment sufficiently clear and well-founded to be the basis of valid and reliable assessment?'; 'What will be the standing of knowledge?'; and 'How can a framework or map of the past be assessed most effectively?'

From theory into practice

Formative assessment: its importance and prospects
Traditionally most teachers have devoted much time to formative assessment. They have generally considered formative assessment to be an important and illuminating part of their work, and have sought to offer constructive and perceptive feedback despite the time consumed by this. The main factor in determining whether such assessment and reporting continues is likely to be the status accorded to teachers' own assessments. In 1987 the announcement that at the heart of the new assessment process in England and Wales there would be nationally prescribed tests, administered by teachers but with the marking and overall assessment externally monitored,[26] encouraged a number of fears. The effects of such a national testing programme, some educationists predicted, would probably include a narrowing of the curriculum, teaching to the tests, more use of didactic teaching methods and a decline in commitment to regular formative assessment.[27] Publication of the TGAT report a year later did much to allay some of these early fears, particularly TGAT's suggestions that a wide range of SATs should be at the heart of the external testing and that teachers' ratings of pupil performance should be used as a fundamental element of the national assessment system.[28]

The TGAT report also advocated that supplementary assessments should be available for children who needed further investigation and that test materials and assessment procedures should be specially arranged for those children with special educational needs who are not deemed able to take the national tests. Thus the TGAT recommendations raised the possibility of SATs and teacher assessment together offering rich possibilities for both summative and formative assessment, based on the best of existing good practice in each subject, including recent GCSE experience. Conclusions about the impact of GCSE must be tentative so early in its life but already research and the reports of HMI have proved illuminating.[29] For instance, it is clear that assessment of work done during the course appeals to teachers' professionalism and increases the validity of the assessment arrangements by measuring more fully than summative tests what pupils know, understand and can do. By increasing the probability that the assessment arrangements do measure what is important, coursework guards against the tendency with public tests to make important that which can be measured and monitored. HMI have also emphasized that coursework provides better opportunities for pupils to demonstrate and receive credit for positive achievement than those offered by end-of-course examinations.[30] Thus it seems that both formal and informal assessment can benefit from GCSE experience, and that assessment by teachers is important for many reasons, including the fact that it enables pupils' knowledge, skills and understanding to be sampled in a variety of contexts and on a number of occasions.

When the National Curriculum assessment arrangements for history are complete it will become clear whether full advantage has been taken of the opportunities created by TGAT, the ERA and GCSE experience to produce assessment tasks and tests which are valid and reliable, to encourage good classroom practice and to support traditional formative assessment. Such assessment informs teachers constantly about their pupils' learning and how it can be nurtured most effectively. If standards are to be raised this kind of assessment must be sustained within the new arrangements. To achieve this it is necessary that the worth of assessments by teachers, both within their daily work and the national assessment arrangements, is acknowledged.

Teacher assessment and SATs

The status of teacher assessment within the National Curriculum is uncertain at the time of writing. Assessment will be by a combination of teacher assessment and SATs, with the main function of SATs being to enable the quality of teacher assessment within a school to be compared with a prescribed national standard. Arrangements for reconciliation are incomplete but it is known that (a) where SATs do not return a level on an attainment target, then the student's level on that target is the level given by teacher assessment; (b) where the results of the teacher assessment and the SAT assessment are the same, then that is the student's level on that attainment target; and (c) where SATs do return a level on an attainment target, and it is not the same as the teacher assessment level, the student's level on that attainment target is the level on the SAT. Thus SAT assessment is 'preferred' to teacher assessment (though there may be an appeal through the agreed mechanism).

Although SAT assessment is thus 'preferred', it is still possible for the Secretary of State to confer high status on teacher assessment through other decisions regarding the new arrangements. Having reconciled the teacher assessment and the SATs for each attainment target, the levels achieved for the attainment targets grouped under each profile component have to be aggregated to achieve a level for that profile component. Where the number of attainment targets is large only a small proportion are likely to be assessed by SAT and, therefore, many of the teacher assessments will be unmodified. On the other hand, where a profile component (PC) consists of a single attainment target (for instance, English PC1 and PC2 and Science PC1) the SAT result is 'preferred'. For history, with only three attainment targets grouped into one profile component, a great deal will depend upon whether there are SATs for all three attainment targets and, particularly if SATs are limited in their coverage, what arrangements are ordered for aggregation. If all the attainment targets are covered by SATs then teacher assessment is effectively obliterated (unless use is made of an appeal mechanism). This, one assumes, would have adverse consequences for teacher morale and traditional formative assessment. If, however, SATs are limited in coverage and aggregation follows the kind of balanced arrangement originally proposed for English PC3 then it seems probable that traditional formative assessment will be sustained and nourished within a new and developing national assessment scheme.[31]

Those who favour use of national tests rather than teacher assessments stress the importance of value for money, reliability and avoiding possible abuse of the scheme. In theory assessment by teachers is more open to abuse than written examinations with external markers but there are counter arguments. Henry Macintosh, for instance, has claimed that in his experience moderation is needed to inspire confidence in standards as much as to standardize.[32] Angela Leonard has supported this view, asserting that as a moderator of history coursework for CSE, Joint O-Level/CSE and GCSE she has found that marks from the vast majority of centres do not require adjustment.[33] Drawing upon research and examination experience, Macintosh, Leonard, and Kingdom and Stobart all support teacher accreditation as a way of reducing moderation procedures to a reasonable level, while also offering positive encouragement to teachers and respect for their professionalism. Financial costs must be considered because teachers will need special training if they are to have full responsibility for assessing their pupils' work in relation to some attainment targets, as well as administering SATs. Moderation procedures will also be costly at first in both time and money, but the benefits in terms of professional development will be considerable and it should be possible to scale down moderating procedures after a few years. More important, however, is the fact that teacher assessment will significantly increase the validity of the assessment scheme. This is particularly relevant now that it has become clear that the time allowed for administering SATs will be much less than was originally envisaged. The time available for SATs for Key Stage 1 has been cut to the equivalent of a week and a half of teaching time and history may be allocated no more than a total of two or three hours. In such circumstances teacher assessment is needed to guarantee the descriptive validity of the national testing arrangements (ie the extent to which an assessment is actually measuring what its descriptive scheme contends it is measuring).

Teaching time and time for assessment
A further requirement is the need to achieve a balance between time for teaching and time for assessment. Public assessment has usually been an event rather than a process, and an event which has hugely disrupted the final term or more. The acceptance of coursework as a component of public assessment has altered the balance somewhat, but for pupils aged between 15–16 and 17–18 in England and Wales most if not all of their final term is lost for teaching as a result of the form and timing of public examinations. When the National Curriculum was introduced there was concern that the statutory testing and reporting in the lower and middle years of schooling might mean the loss of considerable teaching time there too, and that the assessment and reporting edifice being constructed might dominate the work of teachers and schools.[34] Certainly there is a danger of teachers spending so much time carrying out assessments and tabulating the results that lesson preparation and classroom teaching are adversely affected. Conversely, it is also the case that if time for national assessment is very limited then it is likely that tests, not tasks, will be set. This in turn will have implications for content validity and for teaching approaches. It will be important, therefore, to monitor the situation regularly, including the possible teaching time being lost due to assessment requirements, and to take whatever action is necessary.

Above all, there is a need to ensure that really worthwhile use is made of the time available for teaching and assessing history. This use will be shaped by the attainment targets, programmes of study and the statutory assessment arrangements. In 1985 HMI presented a particularly eloquent and persuasive statement of history's potential contribution to the development of pupils and of society, arguing that 'thinking historically strengthens our knowledge and understanding of our memories and gives us procedures to evaluate and learn from them'.[35] Clearly the History Working Group shared this concern that pupils should be equipped with a sound combination of knowledge, skills and understanding.[36] Provided the assessment arrangements encourage the acquisition of skills and understanding as well as knowledge, then history in the National Curriculum should lead to more pupils achieving considerable historical knowledge together with an appreciation of the particular preoccupations and procedures of historical study. Pupils will be equipped with an intellectual cutting edge which should reduce the likelihood of their succumbing to the abuse of history.

Criterion-referenced assessment in history
Another issue is whether the notion of designing criterion-referenced assessments to test attainment targets in history over ten levels of attainment is a feasible one. The perceived advantages of this form of assessment include pupils' achievements being assessed in relation to criteria (not against other students as happens with norm-referencing), and teachers and pupils being aware in advance of the assessment criteria, which should lead to more carefully focused courses and less disparity between the learning processes and assessment. In their Interim Report the History Working Group rightly stressed recent advances in approaches to assessment in history.[37] However, there remains a need to consider whether the attainment targets proposed can be assessed, internally and externally, with an acceptable degree of validity and reliability at the various key stages and, if they can, which particular methods of assessment are most appropriate for each key stage. Desmond Nuttall has warned of various difficulties associated with developing criterion-referenced assessment,[38] and Caroline Gipps has stressed the difficulty of 'describing skills at the different levels in meaningful language so that the difference between levels is clear and unambiguous'.[39]

In history recent experience of criterion-referenced assessment has been both cautionary and positive. For instance, the creation of national criteria for GCSE history meant that syllabuses had thereafter to fulfil the stated criteria and that teachers and students knew for sure

which skills and concepts would be tested. In practice, however, not all
questions have allowed full differentiation. Evidence of potential
problems exists in the experiences of the Grade Related History
Working Party chaired by Martin Booth. He and his colleagues sought
a way of translating GCSE grades into a more detailed statement of
what each candidate had done to achieve his or her grade. Problems
included those of progression, aggregation and breaking down and
specifying appropriate skills and concepts for assessment and reporting
purposes.[40]

One possible approach to solving such problems has been adopted by
the Cambridge History Project (CHP). In this project students' work
centres on six domains reflecting the main skill and concept areas
addressed by the syllabus objectives. (The six domains are 'Historical
enquiry', 'Using sources as evidence', 'Cause and motive', 'Offering
explanations', 'Change and development' and 'Constructing
accounts'.) Each domain has three levels of response, each unit of
assessment specifies which domain is being selected, and the students'
summative profiles of achievement will contain a traditional grade plus
a statement of their performance over the six domains. The pattern of
assessment, which allows for progressive refinement of the indicators, is
explained further in the following extracts from the project's 'Scheme of
assessment';

> Assessment of the levels which students attain will be carried out by
> means of INDICATORS OF ATTAINMENT. These will be statements describing
> levels of attainment *particular to specific questions*, and will be the raw
> material of the mark schemes actually employed in CHP assessments.
> The stock of indicators for any domain will be continuously revised as
> increased experience is acquired in the working of the assessment system
> and as students demonstrate alternative ways of reaching certain levels
> to those predicted by the teacher.[41]

Peter Lee has provided further evidence of interesting new opportunities for teachers and examiners with his suggestion in an earlier chapter
(pages 58–62 'A framework of knowledge') that teaching and assessment of a pupil's developing framework or map of the past could
concentrate on aspects including ability to integrate new material, to
understand connections, to handle different strands within the framework, and to move up and down the temporal scale making long term
links or comparisons. Also on an optimistic note, the development
work for the National Curriculum SATs in the core subjects was

initially funded at a level enabling the agencies involved to undertake extensive trials and to draw widely on available talent and good practice. Arrangements for the development of SATs for the foundation subjects seem certain to be very different but development work and INSET in history should benefit considerably from the experience of levels of response assessment gained through the pioneering work of the Schools History Project and through GCSE and CHP.

Having said all that, there are good reasons for further consideration of some of the reservations and suggestions made by the National Curriculum History Committee for Wales in their final report. In a section on assessment of history within the National Curriculum they state:

> We do not see any problem in identifying ten levels of attainment in history *overall*. Successful GCSE practice already indicates that it is possible to reach a high degree of consensus on the level at which a pupil has demonstrated achievement overall in history. We believe that an aggregated assessment, for the attainment targets taken together within the single profile component, could likewise provide a clear measure of a pupil's achievement in history throughout his or her school career. But ... we are doubtful whether they [teachers] could necessarily and meaningfully differentiate between *ten* distinct levels in each of the attainment targets. We believe that such minute classification of conceptual understanding may be over-elaborate. We are not convinced that teachers could in practice identify such precise gradations with sufficient certainty for them to be meaningfully reported to parents ... We therefore consider that there is a case for having fewer levels within some or all of the attainment targets, or for merging the statements of attainment for some contiguous levels.[42]

A personal opinion is that there may also be good reasons for reporting achievement in a way which brings together for the profile component score the notion of a prescribed number of levels and the use of some simple means (perhaps one or more plus signs) to indicate the number of achievements beyond the reported level. Ideally assessment and reporting should show concern for progression, exactness in measurement and simplicity in reporting. This suggestion might make a small contribution towards the achievement of these requirements.

Recording and reporting of attainment
In July 1989 SEAC recommended that the standardized reports at 7, 11, 14 and 16 should be the only ones required by legislation and warned

that compiling records of achievement would 'place an inescapable demand for resources upon both local authorities and schools, particularly in terms of teachers' time'. In her response the Minister for Schools announced that the government proposed to require annual reports, thus ignoring SEAC's warning about resources. This episode provides further evidence of central government in England controlling decisions on *particulars* as well as overall policy. It also means that teachers now have a legal duty to record and report annually on each pupil's level of attainment for each of the attainment targets. Time and expertise are required if the process of assessment and recording is to be fair, sensitive and valid. For the teacher of younger children there is the problem of assessing and recording the achievements of possibly 30 children in eight or nine subjects. (One calculation is that a teacher with a class of 30 pupils who is responsible for their work in just the core subjects of English, mathematics and science will have to consider a possible 6,810 statements of attainment.) Secondary school history teachers are likely to have direct responsibility for at least 200 pupils, possibly 300 or more. If they have 200 pupils and spend five minutes per week per pupil after school – reading each pupil's work, evaluating and commenting upon it, and up-dating their records – that amounts to a total of nearly 17 hours per week. If they have 300 pupils it means 25 hours per week or three and a half hours per night, seven days per week! Would parents and pupils consider that five minutes per week is sufficient to do the task properly?

The DES in a document on teachers' pay and conditions published in spring 1989 emphasized that recording and reporting children's progress are part of a teacher's contractual obligation, stating 'the teacher shall ... work such additional hours as may be needed to discharge effectively his (sic) professional duties including ... the writing of reports'. In fairness to teachers there is now an urgent need to calculate the time that should be allocated for assessment, record-keeping and reporting, though sadly it is likely that one outcome of such an initiative will be a reduction in the day-by-day assessment that has helped most children (but has lengthened considerably the working day of every conscientious teacher). Perhaps this is the moment to investigate whether responding to all or most of pupils' classwork and homework is essential for effective teaching and learning, or whether the occasional statutory testing and assessment is sufficient to raise standards or at least to keep them at present levels. If, as seems probable, a combination of pervasive formative assessment and the new statutory system is the arrangement most likely to bring higher standards of learning then a supplementary study should be made of the implications for teachers' time (and remuneration).

Two further aspects that require thorough consideration and monitoring are what should be recorded on a pupil's report, and how should attainment be reported to parents? Should achievements be reported only in relation to attainment targets or should other achievements be mentioned too? Should pupils have an opportunity for self-assessment? Should detailed information be supplied about each attainment target, or the aggregated result? If levels of attainment are aggregated then much information will be lost; if full details plus the aggregated result are given then assertions of injustice are certain to arise.

This is because if, as proposed at present, the profile component is the unit for public reporting and the level for that component is the highest level attained or exceeded by the pupil in not less than half the attainment targets, then one pupil would be awarded a profile component score of 3 as a result of achieving, for instance, levels 1, 2, 2, 3, 3, 3 whereas another pupil would be awarded a profile score of 2 for achieving levels 2, 2, 2, 2, 4, 5. Similarly two pupils scoring 1, 3, 1, 1, 3, 3 and 3, 4, 3, 3, 3, 4 respectively would be awarded the same profile score. The public reporting of results is also likely to lead to other unintended but very important outcomes. One of these is likely to be an increase in staffing problems in some areas. Following the publication of the TGAT Report, which stated that 'the publication of school results . . . would be liable to lead to complacency if results were adjusted, and to misinterpretation if they are not',[43] it was decided that results at school level should be reported in unadjusted form. Although the TGAT report recommended that any report by a school which includes national assessment results should 'include a general report for the area, prepared by the local authority, to indicate the nature of socio-economic and other influences which are known to affect schools',[44] it seems likely that one outcome of the publication of unadjusted results will be a further haemorrhage of experienced staff from maintained schools in many inner-city and deprived areas.

Some suggestions for good assessment practice

The issues and questions explored in this section indicate the importance of assessment, record-keeping and reporting as agents of change, the demands that they make on teachers' time, and the need to establish a list of criteria that they should satisfy. The suggestions below offer ten points arising from the discussion here in the hope that they may encourage others to debate the assumptions underlying each one and to develop criteria and guidelines in relation to national assessment arrangements which will help to ensure that changes become real gains.

- Public assessment should measure what is important in terms of pupils' learning in history, not make what is easily measurable important.
- Assessment arrangements should reflect and not constrain good teaching and learning in history.
- Assessment should be an integral part of the educational process, not simply a bolt-on addition at the end of a course.
- Formal assessment should measure the stated objective of the history curriculum; it should also be fair, reliable and positive.
- Assessment arrangements should be not only capable of measuring what they seek to measure but also appropriate to the age and ability of the pupils, and to the particular concept, skill or attainment target being assessed.
- Whatever techniques or activities form the vehicle for assessment, recording should be precise and systematic, and reporting should provide a clear and informative description of attainment.
- Moderation procedures should encourage history teachers to discuss work submitted and the teaching strategies and curricular organization that gave rise to them (ideally through contacts between schools in consortia).
- There should be trials of a range of activities, oral and practical as well as written, that might be employed to judge attainment in order to establish their value and weaknesses.
- A national assessment system should value assessments by history teachers and have a positive impact on formative and diagnostic assessment.
- Assessment, in all its forms, should not encroach too much on teaching time or teachers' time.

Conclusion

The main educational aim behind the national assessment system created by the ERA is to improve standards of teaching and learning in schools. Certainly assessment can aid the achievement of this aim. It can focus attention on objectives, encourage continuity and progression in the curriculum, inform parents about the progress of their children, and provide all interested parties with more information than hitherto about the achievements of each maintained school. Assessment can also, as stressed earlier, bring further understanding and satisfaction to both teachers and pupils. Conversely, it can interrupt the learning process and in some circumstances result in the imposition of excessive pressure on teachers and pupils. In the past summative assessment, particularly in the final years of secondary schooling, has led to an emphasis on covering content to the detriment of understanding, as well as the loss of considerable teaching time. Use of attainment targets, statements of attainment and national testing could prove to be a watershed, providing an unprecedented amount of data about what children can do in history from the ages of 5 to 16. This data could lead to welcome advances in our knowledge of what pupils can achieve in history, their learning difficulties, how best to overcome them and the general effectiveness of different teaching techniques. The new system could stimulate more action research and aid professional development in various ways. Alternatively it could lead to a much narrower education than hitherto for pupils aged 5 to 16 while also imposing demands and pressures on teachers that sap their morale and professionalism. Certainly the new system will decide the nature and future of history in education in England and Wales.

Teachers, politicians, parents and the wider community all have a responsibility to provide pupils with the best education that is possible. Through the ERA, politicians have radically reshaped the framework within which teachers and pupils must work in maintained schools in England and Wales. Ultimately it is the soundness of that framework and the skill and motivation of teachers that will determine whether the changes will lead to genuine gains for pupils. Assessment arrangements are the keystone of the framework. In order to achieve genuine gains rather than simply changes it is necessary to monitor and amend the assessment arrangements in accord with the best information and advice available. It is surely also necessary to sustain the morale and professionalism of teachers, not least by ensuring that assessment of pupil performance by teachers – both formal and informal – is fully recognized as a really important element of a national assessment system.

Notes

1. I am indebted to Humberto Pereira Mafra for this extract from his teaching practice log.
2. These arrangements are outlined more fully in DES (1989a), *From Policy to Practice*. London: HMSO.

3. Wragg, T. (1989), 'When testing can become a tyranny'. *The Observer*, 30 July 1989.

4. Ibid.

5. HMSO (1988), *Education Reform Act*. London: HMSO.

6. DES and Welsh Office (1988a), *Task Group on Assessment and Testing: A Report*. London: HMSO. Later in the same year three supplementary reports were published; DES and Welsh Office (1988b), *Task Group on Assessment and Testing Report: Three Supplementary Reports*. London: HMSO.

7. The full text of the Secretary of State's announcement is printed in DES and Welsh Office (1989a), *English for Ages 5 to 16: Proposals of the Secretary of State for Education and the Secretary of State for Wales*. London: HMSO/NCC, Appendix 4.

8. HMSO (1988), op. cit., section 14. The general functions of SEAC are also stated in DES (1989a), op. cit., Annex A2.

9. Paragraph 12 of the Supplementary Guidance to the Chairman of the History Working Group. For the complete terms of reference and supplementary guidance to the chairperson see DES and Welsh Office (1989b), *National Curriculum History Working Group Interim Report*. London: HMSO (pp. 103–9); or DES and Welsh Office (April 1990), *National Curriculum History Working Group Final Report*. London: HMSO (pp. 187–191).

10. DES and Welsh Office (April 1990), op. cit., (p. 7, para. 3.8).

11. HCA, 'Submission by the History Curriculum Association to the Secretary of State on the Final Report of the History Working Group'. PO Box 682, Lewes, East Sussex, BN8 6LW.

12. DES (July 1990), *History for ages 5 to 16: Proposals of the Secretary of State for Education and Science*. London: HMSO/NCC (pp. iii–iv).

13. Lomas, T.(1990), 'How appropriate is the model proposed by the Task Group on Assessment and Testing (TGAT) for history?'. Unpublished discussion paper. Dr Tim Lomas, Education Inspector (History), Lincolnshire LEA, was a co-opted member of the National Curriculum History Working Group.

14. DES and Welsh Office (1988a), op. cit., para. 175.

15. DES and Welsh Office (1988b), op. cit. (pp. 20–1).

16. For instance, Shemilt, D. (1987), 'Adolescent ideas about evidence and methodology in history', and Ashby, R. and Lee, P. (1987), 'Children's concepts of empathy and understanding in history'. In: C. Portal (ed.), *The History Curriculum for Teachers*. Lewes: The Falmer Press. Shemilt, D. (1980), *History 13–16: Evaluation Study*, Edinburgh: Holmes McDougall, remains a seminal study on the development of children's ideas about history.

17. DES (1989b), *Aspects of Primary Education: The Teaching and Learning of History and Geography*. London: HMSO, (p.8, para.11). For evidence of

the state of history in later years too see DES and Welsh Office. (1989b), op.cit. (pp. 6–9).

18. DES (1990), *Standards in Education 1988–1989: The Annual Report of HM Senior Chief Inspector of Schools*. London: DES, London SE1 7PH, (p. 1, para. 5).

19. DES (1989a), op. cit., section 6.2.

20. Ibid., section 5.2.

21. For instance, on 20 August 1989 Judith Judd (in *The Observer*) reported that the Prime Minister, at the time of a Cabinet reshuffle in late July 1989, had overridden the wishes of her former Secretary of State for Education (Kenneth Baker) concerning the formal response to the History Working Group's Interim Report. The Prime Minister, the front page article asserted, had told the new Secretary of State for Education (John MacGregor) to insist that in the group's Final Report there should be more emphasis on British history, on chronology and on factual knowledge. This story may be based on speculation rather than fact, though an article in *The Sunday Telegraph* (9 July 1989), under the headline 'Baker supports New History', reported that the then Secretary of State was about to welcome the Interim Report and considered that it did not require alteration. What is certain is that the letter finally sent to the chairman of the Working Group by John MacGregor, on 10 August 1989, contained six paragraphs raising major issues that the Working Group were asked to consider further. By implication, it rejected possibly the most important recommendation and one supported by the National Curriculum History Committee for Wales, that factual knowledge should be prescribed through the programmes of study and not the attainment targets.

22. John MacGregor's letter in DES and Welsh Office (1989b), op.cit.

23. Commander Saunders Watson's letter prefacing DES and Welsh Office (1989b), op. cit.

24. Johnson-Laird, P.N. and Wason, P.C. (1977), 'A theoretical analysis of insight into a reasoning task'. In: P.N. Johnson-Laird and P.C. Wason (eds), *Thinking: Readings in Cognitive Science*. Cambridge: Cambridge University Press.

25. Dickinson, A.K. (1984), 'Assessment, examinations and historical understanding'. In: A.K. Dickinson, P.J. Lee and P.J. Rogers (eds), *Learning History*. London: Heinemann Educational Books.

26. DES and Welsh Office (1987), *The National Curriculum 5–16: A Consultative Document*. London: HMSO, (p.11).

27. See, for instance, Gipps, C. (1988), 'The TGAT report: trick or treat'. In: *Forum*, Vol. 31, No. 1.

28. DES and Welsh Office (1988a), op. cit., para. 60.

29. For research findings see, for instance, Kingdom, M. and Stobart, G. (1988), *GCSE Examined*. Lewes: The Falmer Press; DES (1988), *Report by HM Inspectors on the Introduction of the General Certificate of Secondary*

Education in Schools, 1986-1988. London: DES Publications, based on the observation by HMI of approximately 2,000 lessons.

30. DES (1988), op. cit.

31. The Secretary of State's Order of July 1990 for aggregation for English PC3 (Writing) at key stage 1 states that if the levels of AT4 (spelling) and AT5 (handwriting) are both below the level of AT3 (writing), then the level on the profile component is the higher of the levels AT4 and AT5. Otherwise the level on the profile component is the level on AT3.

32. Macintosh, H. (1986), 'The sacred cows of coursework'. In: C. Gipps (ed.), *The GCSE: an uncommon examination.* Bedford Way Papers 29, University of London Institute of Education.

33. Leonard, A. (1989), 'The implications of assessed coursework in GCSE'. Unpublished research paper.

34. See, for instance, Judd, J., 'Maggie's monster tests the patience'. In: *The Observer*, 3 September 1989. Also, Wilby, P., 'A prescription worse than the disease'. In: *The Independent*, 23 March 1989.

35. DES (1985), *History in the Primary and Secondary Years: An HMI View.* London: HMSO, (p. 40).

36. See, for instance, DES and Welsh Office (1989b), op. cit., para. 2.2.

37. Ibid., para. 6.7.

38. Nuttall, D. (1987), 'Testing, testing, testing'. In: *NUT Education Review.* Vol.1, No.2.

39. Gipps, C. (1988), op. cit. (pp. 6–7). For a recent criticism of the notion of 'levels' and 'stages' of learning see Goldstein, H. and Noss, R. (1990), 'Against the stream'. In: *Forum*, Vol. 33, No. 1.

40. Ben Jones, R. (1986), 'Grade criteria: opportunity or impending disaster'. *Teaching History*, No. 44, February 1986.

41. See 'Scheme of assessment'. In: *Cambridge Advanced Level History Project Examination Syllabuses for 1990 and 1991.* University of Cambridge Local Examinations Syndicate, Cambridge CB1 2EU.

42. The Welsh Office (July 1990), *National Curriculum History Committee for Wales Final Report.* Wales: HMSO, (p. 133).

43. DES and Welsh Office (1988a), op. cit., para. 133.

44. Ibid., Recommendation 31.

Chapter Five
The Historical Dimension

Richard Aldrich and Dennis Dean

Introduction

This final chapter is concerned to place the contemporary debate about the place of history in the National Curriculum in its historical context. It is natural and proper that historians should approach this issue in an historical way. As David Cannadine has recently argued: 'If we do not think historically about our own problems, we can hardly expect anyone else to think historically about theirs.'[1] This responsibility rests particularly upon those, like ourselves, who have been professionally engaged in both the history of education and the training of history teachers. In this chapter to think (and indeed to write) historically is taken to mean the collection of historical evidence about the teaching of history, and the formation of reasoned judgements based upon such evidence. Such an approach must require, as far as is possible, the eschewing of contemporary personal positions, whether in respect of party political affiliation or commitment to particular projects for the teaching of history. It does not, however, necessitate the abandonment of theoretical analysis nor of the use of insights drawn from other social sciences.

The theoretical starting point for this chapter is that the formal curricula of schools, of which history now forms an integral part, are the product of interaction between and among individuals and groups.[2] Such interaction involves conflict and co-operation which reflect a variety of factors: for example, personal and group self-interest, political, social and educational theories and policies. Thus those who are employed to study and teach history can, almost without exception, be relied upon to argue the case for their subject interest; just as geographers, mathematicians, physical educationists and others, will have similar commitments to the advancement, in all senses of the word, of their own fields of learning. Within any particular subject or field, moreover, there will be further interest groups making for intra-subject, as well as inter-subject, conflict and co-operation. Medieval history may be championed against modern history, political and constitutional history against social and economic, history from above against history from below, history as fact against history as skills.

Individuals and interest groups in education, however, include not only the teachers, but also the providers and consumers – central and local government, employers, the general public, parents, students and pupils. Such groups are not likely to be as convinced of the value of history as are those who teach it. Indeed there is considerable evidence to show that schoolchildren, parents and employers do not regard the subject of history as being particularly useful in promoting basic or vocational skills.[3] In recent years such perceptions have contributed to the relative decline of history in the formal school curriculum.

Although the work of history teachers, and the priorities of pupils, parents and employers are of immense importance in determining the standing of the subject in schools, from an historical viewpoint government policy has probably been the most important single factor. In 1990 the power of central government in curriculum matters in England and Wales is greater than it has been for decades, and may prove to be greater than ever before. At first sight it would appear that historians should welcome the National Curriculum, for it has ensured the place of the subject throughout the years of compulsory schooling. But the introduction of history into the National Curriculum has provoked conflict, rather than co-operation, between central government and some groups of history teachers, and among historians themselves. Such conflict has arisen not over the amount of history to be taught and studied in schools, but over the nature and purpose of such history.

On 10 February 1984 the then Secretary of State for Education, Keith Joseph, declared that 'I am clear that history is an essential component in the curriculum of *all* pupils.'[4] Such a statement, delivered as part of a speech to a conference convened by the Historical Association, and the speaker's sensitive and informed responses to the questions raised thereafter were widely appreciated. The Association, however, was less sanguine about the approach of his successor and, shortly after the new Secretary of State took office, an editorial in *Teaching History* concluded by asking Kenneth Baker, 'What will you do to maintain the position of history as the central pivot in the life of a questioning, concerned and tolerant society?'[5] A series of pamphlets, by Beattie,

Deuchar and Kedourie,[6] fiercely attacked a number of elements in school history teaching, including the Schools History Project and the General Certificate of Secondary Education. The possibility of conflict between the Secretary of State and some history teachers was confirmed by a speech delivered on 23 January 1987 at a conference of the Society of Education Officers. Mr Baker informed his audience 'that history was one subject which is causing me growing concern as I learn more about what pupils are actually being taught'.[7]

One of Mr Baker's concerns, it would appear, was that history lessons were being used to challenge rather than to buttress the existing social, economic and political order, and that children were not learning about their heritage. In October 1988, in a speech to the Conservative party conference he announced his determination to ensure that in the future all children would learn the key events in British history, and gave examples. These included: the establishment of the Anglican Church in the sixteenth century; the development of Parliament in the seventeenth; the industrial revolution of the later eighteenth; the extension of the franchise, and 'the spread of Britain's influence for good throughout the world'. 'We should not be ashamed of our history', he concluded, 'our pride in our past gives us our confidence to stand tall in the world today.'[8]

Such assurances were well received by his audience but, understandably, created concern among some history teachers. Did such a statement mean that the precise content of the curriculum would be determined directly by the Secretary of State? Was school history to be cast in an essentially celebratory nationalist or imperialist mould?

Foundations
There are few absolute starting points in history, but the position of history itself in the curriculum of English schools, and the relationship of central government to that position, has a history which is at least one hundred years old. In the nineteenth century the relationship centred upon the public elementary schools. In a survey chapter such as this it is impossible to do justice to the full subtleties of this relationship. At times central government actions increased the amount of history in schools, on other occasions they diminished it. Neither in the nineteenth nor in the twentieth centuries was there any simple line of development.

In the second half of the nineteenth century governmental control of the elementary school curriculum was exercised principally through a system of grants. The most famous (or infamous) system was 'payment by results', inaugurated in 1862 under the terms of the Revised Code.

Grants were paid to schools in accordance with the attainment levels achieved by pupils in annual examinations in the 3Rs (reading, writing and arithmetic) which, together with needlework for girls and religion for all, became the staple curriculum fare. How much history was being taught in elementary schools before 1862 is not clear, but the Annual Report of the Committee of Council for 1865–6 acknowledged that: 'The Revised Code has tended, at least temporarily, to discourage attention to the higher branches of elementary instruction: Geography, Grammar, History.'[9] In this respect it is interesting to note that regulations issued for implementation of the Minute of 25th August 1846, which established the pupil-teacher system, required the pupil-teachers to study a considerable amount of geography and grammar, but very little history. Geography and grammar were required for entry to the apprenticeship, and progress in these areas was examined by the inspectors throughout the five years. In contrast only at the end of their third year were pupil-teachers to be examined in 'the outlines of British history'.[10]

Nevertheless, some history was still taught, and a Minute of 1867 gave schools a financial inducement to do so, when grants were offered for performance in 'specific' subjects. In 1872, geography was by far the most popular specific subject, taken by 59,774 pupils, followed by grammar with 18,426, and history with 16,465. By 1875, though history numbers had risen to 17,710, it had been pushed into fourth place by English literature.[11] In 1875 a new category of 'class' subjects (tested not on the proficiency of individuals but on the performance of the class as a whole) was introduced. Once again history lagged behind geography. Figures from 1890 for the senior classes in which these subjects were taught showed 12,367 taking geography, and only 414 history, although by 1895 this latter figure had increased to 3,597.[12]

Payment by results ended in 1895, and henceforth teachers had more freedom in curricular matters. Nevertheless central government still maintained an overall control, and the Elementary Code of 1900 supplied a list of subjects which schools were expected to teach 'as a rule', a list which included history.

Under the payment-by-results system, children were examined upon their performance upon a prescribed syllabus. Such prescription was necessary if standards were to be consistently applied. The prescribed syllabus for history was concerned exclusively with England:

Standard IV   Outlines of the history of England to the Norman
               Conquest.

Standard V   Outlines of the history of England from the Norman
              Conquest to the accession of Henry VII.
Standard VI   Outlines of the history of England from Henry VII to the
              death of George III.

There can be little doubt that much history teaching under the Revised
Code was concerned with the memorization of facts and dates, but not
all teachers were convinced of the worth of this approach. For example
in 1876 Revd D R Fearon, an experienced Inspector (who was himself
convinced of the importance of knowing historical dates), reported that
'Many teachers pooh-pooh dates . . . This doctrine is a consequence of
the reaction against the old-fashioned method of teaching history . . . by
making the children learn little else than dates.'[13] There were also heated
debates on such issues as bias in textbooks. For example both the
Birmingham and London school boards were involved in controversies
over religious bias in history textbooks. The limitations of many of the
standard works were well understood, and in 1873 the *Educational
Times* found such great difficulty in recommending impartial history
textbooks that it urged 'the oral system of teaching, preferring to leave
the matter in the hands of the master to adopting any of the existing
objectionable textbooks on the subject'.[14]

In the twentieth century central government acknowledged the role
of teachers in determining the syllabuses and teaching methods of the
elementary school. The Board of Education's *Handbook of Suggestions
for the Consideration of Teachers and others engaged in the Work of
Public Elementary Schools*, first issued in 1905, declared that the only
uniformity of practice which the Board wished to see in elementary
schools was that 'each teacher shall think for himself, and work out for
himself such methods of teaching as may use his powers to the best
advantage and be best suited to the particular needs and conditions of
the school'.[15]

Such freedom was considered to be particularly appropriate to
history teachers. The Board's Report for 1910-11 advised that 'in the
long run success or failure in History teaching, more perhaps than in
any other subject, depends upon the ability and interest of the
individual teacher'.[16] By the later 1920s the *Handbook of Suggestions*
advised that teachers should first consider 'what children can understand', and that:

The history syllabus, even for schools in similar circumstances, may
properly vary according to the capacity and interests of the teacher. It is

undesirable that all schools in any particular locality should follow precisely the same syllabus. Each teacher should think out and frame his own scheme, having regard to the circumstances of his own school, its rural or urban environment, its staffing and classification, and in some measure also to the books and the topics which most appeal to him.[17]

Whereas the School Boards established in 1870 were responsible only for elementary education, the LEAs which came into being in 1902 were empowered to provide secondary schools as well. In 1904 the Board of Education issued secondary school regulations which laid down overall curricula for such schools, with history as one of the compulsory subjects. Though the minimum amount of time to be allotted to each subject or group of subjects was to last a mere three years, the regulations, even as late as 1935, were quite specific about the compulsory subjects of study.[18] Thus a curriculum was established for the twentieth-century secondary school, a curriculum which largely survived the demise of the grammar school and, with minor modifications, is that prescribed under the 1988 Act for all children aged 5–16 in state schools.

In the first half of the twentieth century, however, in secondary as in elementary or primary schools no rigid historical syllabus was prescribed by central government. Board of Education Circular 599 on the teaching of history, issued in 1908, declared history to be a subject 'in which perhaps more than in any other there is room for the greatest variety of treatment',[19] and indicated the variety of syllabuses and approaches in existence. But the Board's recommendations, the introduction of the Certificate Examination in 1917, and the choices of teachers themselves, crystallized into a broadly chronological treatment with a detailed study of modern English and European history for examination purposes. By the early 1950s some three-quarters of grammar schools were following a history course which comprised:[20]

Age 11–12	Pre-history, ancient civilizations, or medieval history
Age 12–13	The Tudors and Stuarts
Age 13–14	The eighteenth century in England, with some American and Empire history and sometimes the eighteenth century in Europe
Age 14–15 }	Nineteenth-century English and European history (occa-
Age 15–16 }	sionally American) to be taken for the certificate examination.

As central government control over the school curriculum declined, 'official' policy on history teaching came to be represented by pamphlets issued by the Ministry of Education. Pamphlet 23, an influential publication of some 90 pages, indicated the growing importance of 'patch' history (study in depth), and its capacity to promote empathy or, in the terminology of the 1950s, 'a quality of sympathetic imagination . . . a humility about one's own age and the things to which one is accustomed, a willingness to enter into a different experience.'[21]

Since no coherent or detailed curricular policy on issues such as the nature and content of history teaching could be expected from the more than 300 LEAs established under the 1902 Act and as central direction declined, so history became a matter for historians and history teachers, both as individuals, and as interest groups. It is important, therefore to trace the origins of what might be called the histoᵣical profession.

The general apparatus of modern historical study and the creation of a substantial body of professional historians took shape in England, as in many other countries, at the end of the nineteenth century. The *English Historical Review* was founded in 1886. Honours history schools were established at Oxford and Cambridge in the 1870s, and history departments also appeared in the new university colleges and universities founded in the later nineteenth and early twentieth centuries. Thus an academic historical establishment came into being. Though the overall numbers of university history tutors and students were low in comparison with those of today, their influence was considerable. For example, by 1928 one-quarter of Cambridge undergraduates were studying history.[22] History was no longer merely an adjunct of Classics, or an appendage of literature, but had established itself as a high status subject in its own right, seen as being a particularly suitable study for those who intended to embark upon careers in politics, public service at home or in the empire, in the élite professions, or simply as ladies and gentlemen.

In addition to the academic historians, another significant group emerged whose professional status, while depending in part upon their ability to teach the subject in schools, was firmly based upon their formal qualifications as historians. Many, indeed, had no formal training as teachers. These were the graduate history masters and mistresses in independent and élite grammar schools. The views of several of the male members of this group were represented in the publications of the Incorporated Association of Assistant Masters, notably the *Memorandum on the Teaching of History* of 1925, and the several editions of *The Teaching of History*, first produced in 1950. The *Memorandum*, which drew upon the experience of a panel of 74 history teachers, contrasted such wisdom with what was often seen as the baneful influence of university dons, inspectors and examination boards. The book published in 1950, which like the 1925 memorandum was actually produced by a committee of 12 schoolmasters, declared that the history master should be 'a man of vigorous and lucid intellect, imaginative as well as analytical . . . his culture should be wide, in literature and in the arts and in humanity, he should be widely travelled.'[23] The third edition of 1965 placed particular emphasis upon the teacher as researcher and writer: 'The self discipline of writing will bring him rich rewards; his own scholarship will be revived, and he will be reminded of the difficulties inherent in the practice of his craft.'[24]

Such interest groups among the profession were overarched, though not overshadowed, by the Historical Association, founded in 1906. It was not the first of the subject associations; the Mathematical Association had been founded as early as 1870, the Classical Association as recently as 1903. The initiative proceeded from two members of the History department of the London Day Training College (from 1932 the University of London Institute of Education), who became the first honorary secretaries of the Association, Miss M A Howard and Dr Rachel Reid.

Howard's vision was expressed on 5 January 1906 to a conference of elementary schoolteachers chaired by Professor A F Pollard of University College, London. She outlined an association which might fulfil three ends: to keep those teaching in schools in touch with the work being done in universities; to bring pressure (when necessary) to bear on educational authorities and on examining bodies; to co-ordinate the efforts of all who were working towards the improvement of school history teaching.[25] The composition of the Association's first Council indicated the nature of such co-operation. There were some eleven university members, nine from secondary schools, and four from teacher-training institutions.

Membership, initially open to 'all persons engaged or interested in the teaching of history', was widened in 1917 to include 'all persons interested in the study and teaching of history'; thus professional and lay interests might be joined together. This change contributed towards a rapid increase in membership in the years following the First World War; from 1,524 members and 382 associates in 1918–19, to 4,738 members with 826 associates in 1922–3. Numbers remained fairly constant during the inter-war period, fell during the Second World

War, but increased to over 8,000 by 1950.[26] In 1990 it stands at some 7,000.

Thus it can be seen that by the 1950s history was an established subject in schools and in higher education. Neither central nor local government was exercising specific control over the actual form and content of the historical syllabuses. Interest groups had arisen which reflected the hierarchical nature of English professional society. Though in theory there might be freedom for history teachers in schools to select, even to construct their own syllabuses, in fact there was considerable uniformity. Such uniformity stemmed from the general acceptance of two guiding principles. The first was that since history was the study of human events through the dimension of time a chronological approach was natural. The second was the centrality of British, or even English, history, though the limitations of such history encouraged, in secondary schools at least, some acquaintance with the 'ancient world' for younger pupils, and with continental Europe for older ones. Such principles were reflected in textbooks and in the syllabuses of external examining bodies.

Nevertheless, in spite of such hierarchies and uniformities, rationales as to *why* history should be taught were very varied indeed. It is important to examine the historical foundations of such differences because they lie at the heart of the present disputes. Throughout the twentieth century history has been studied for a variety of purposes. These include: the study of history 'for its own sake'; as a means of social control; to introduce children to their heritage; to promote moral virtue; to inculcate civic pride and patriotism; to foster a love of peace and international understanding; to develop a variety of skills, both of a general, and of a specifically historical, nature. It is impossible to examine all of these in depth here,[27] and they were not necessarily mutually exclusive. It is clear that the rationales reflected the particular interests, ideals and beliefs both of individuals and of groups. The prominence, or indeed prevalence of one rationale over others, frequently reflected the political and social priorities of the contemporary scene.

History's place in the public and grammar schools, and in the ancient universities, stemmed particularly from the long-held belief, expressed in the eighteenth century by Lord Chesterfield to his son, that 'An intimate knowledge of history, my dear boy, is absolutely necessary for the legislator, the orator and the statesman.'[28] History was valued as a storehouse of experience for those who would lead and govern the nation, and the study of political and constitutional history was particularly valuable for this task. But history was not only important in inculcating qualities of leadership, it was also useful in promoting followership. For most of the twentieth century school history has been presented within an anodyne, ameliorist framework. Rob Gilbert has shown how English history, as taught in schools, has been explained as a success story which has been to the mutual benefit of all its citizens. History has been employed 'to explain the process by which individual agents and social change have addressed and largely solved the problems of equality, opportunity, mobility and material welfare'.[29]

Thus although history may have been explained in different ways for different social classes, it has also been employed as a unifying agent, as a social cement, and never more so than in times of acute national crisis. As a result heritage, patriotism, imperialism, and the superior virtues of British democracy found particular expression when the nation was at war. During the First World War leading historians, for example Hugh Egerton and C R L Fletcher, contributed to the series of Oxford pamphlets which sought to explain to the British public and others why, historically speaking, Germany had no right to covet Britain's empire. During the Second World War historians were employed to fulfil the same function. In 1940 in addressing the Historical Association, C M MacInnes, Reader in Imperial History at the University of Bristol, assured his audience that the historical record showed 'that we are better fitted than Nazi Germany or than any other totalitarian state to govern backward races and to help them along the difficult paths of civilisation'.[30]

On the other hand the immediate years after the First World War were notable for attempts to use historical study and teaching to promote international understanding. In 1921 a history subcommittee of the Education Committee of the League of Nations Union was established in Britain. By 1925 the Association of Education Committees was circularizing its 250 members with suggestions for promoting the ideals of the League. In 1927 H A L Fisher, the distinguished historian and former president of the Board of Education, declared that the League of Nations and its ideals should be taught in history lessons.[31] In 1933 Walter Harte, president of the Historical Association, and C W Kimmins, chairman of the Education Committee of the Union, were among the contributors to the *Educational Survey* published by the League in Geneva. Their main purpose was to refute accusations that history teaching in Britain was largely based on patriotism, and to provide evidence to the contrary.[32] Similarly, after 1945, a series of Unesco conferences and a spate of publications sought to eradicate bias, to promote tolerance, to improve textbooks, to increase international understanding, and to see British history (including imperial history) through others' eyes.[33]

It is important to notice, however, that although events of the magnitude of world wars naturally affected attitudes towards history teaching, and led to different ideologies at particular periods, nevertheless one can trace certain continuities. There has been a steady move away from the English-history-centred curriculum of the nineteenth-century elementary school, which has received support both in peace and war from history professionals and from government officials. Thus in 1944 the Historical Association's influential pamphlet, *The Planning of a History Syllabus for Schools*, concluded that the main history course for pupils aged 11 to 16 should be 'one of European History expanding into World History with constant reference to, and illustration from, English, or rather British, History'. Such a general course should be supplemented by detailed study of a special subject or period, the principal purpose of which should be to give the pupils 'some skill in collecting, arranging, and interpreting historical evidence for themselves'.[34]

In 1967 the Department of Education and Science issued a pamphlet entitled *Towards World History* which, while cautious in tone and repudiating any wish to 'abandon' British history altogether, called for the development of 'a new relationship between British history and that of the world as a whole'.[35]

Finally, in this section, it is important to consider another long-standing rationale for the teaching of history, namely that of teaching history as a process. Historical method – the collection of evidence, and the formation of judgements based upon such evidence, free from bias and irrational prejudice – is a skill which is both essential for the historian and for any citizen in a democratic society.

Some of the early observers and exponents of the source method of history teaching were cautious in their claims. In 1902 H E Bourne warned that 'the pupils should not be allowed to entertain the flattering notion that they are doing what historians have been obliged to do, except as the infant toddles in the path run by the athlete'.[36] Similarly M W Keatinge, author of the highly influential *Studies in the Teaching of History*, 1910, and *A History of England for Schools with Documents, Problems and Exercises*, 1911, who sought to introduce pupils to the methods of the modern scientific historian, and to emphasize the capacity of the subject for promoting rigorous thought, advised that 'The boy is no more placed in the position of the historian who weighs and estimates his raw material than the boy in the laboratory who is being put through a course of practical work...is being placed in the position of the scientific discoverer'.[37]

By the late 1920s, however, larger claims were being made. F C Happold, whose *Approach to History* was published in 1928, entered a 'plea for the substitution of historical training for the mere teaching of history in schools'.[38] He outlined a course in which 'emphasis is placed not so much on the acquisition of historical knowledge as of correct methods of work and of a capacity for historical thinking'.[39] In the following year Catherine Firth, in a chapter on historical method in *The Learning of History in Elementary Schools*, declared that 'The search for evidence, the framing of hypotheses, their testing, their verification, modification or rejection',[40] was a process which was common to the student in the Public Record Office, the teacher working out a fresh lesson for a class, and the child who was writing an answer to a 'thinking question'.

The 1930s saw a powerful counter-attack against the emphasis upon the use of historical evidence and the promotion of historical thinking by children. As war clouds gathered the nation looked to its moral and patriotic defences. The emphasis on historical process was challenged, and history teachers were urged 'to give precedence to ethical over intellectual values'.[41] In 1939 M V C Jeffreys concluded his argument for the line of development approach to the teaching of history with a section on 'social studies' and 'education for citizenship'.[42]

Two conclusions therefore may be drawn at this point. The first is that over a period of 100 years from the 1860s central government was the major power in deciding how much history should be taught in schools, both at the elementary and at the secondary levels. The second is that the nature of that history was determined by the aims and objectives of certain groups – governments, examination boards, historians, teachers – which differed not only according to the interests of such groups, but also according to political, economic and educational circumstances.

Recent changes

Change and continuity are the essence of history. From the 1960s the pace and extent of changes in Britain increased, both in education and in society at large. Changes in higher education were prompted by the Robbins report of 1963. Changes in secondary schools centred upon the development of the comprehensive system, particularly after the issue of Circular 10/65. Changes in the primary schools were epitomized by the Plowden report of 1967.

Broader societal changes included the end of empire, the accelerating decline of Britain as a world power in both political and economic terms, the abandonment of many traditions, the advent of the contraceptive pill, the rebirth of the feminist movement, the development of a popular teenage culture which found particular expression in popular music, renewed manifestations of nationalism in Scotland, Wales and Ulster, a faltering entry into the European community, and the advent to these shores of peoples of other races and faiths, principally from lands formerly colonized by Britain.

Such changes were bound to be reflected in the responses of historians and teachers, just as they were in the responses of other groups in society. A new awareness of the present and of the future necessitated a new awareness of the past. Three issues which achieved particular prominence were those of race, gender and class.

Thus, in respect of race, emphasis might be placed not only upon the achievements but also upon the misdeeds and harmful effects of Britain's imperial past. True, the British took peace, railways and Christianity to many parts of the world, but at the same time they frequently justified the empire in terms of racial superiority, and denied or diminished the history, culture, religion, and language of those whom they conquered, and inhibited their social and economic development. True, in the year 1833, slavery was abolished in the British Empire, but for how many years had it existed? How important had its contribution been to the wealth of such cities as Bristol and Liverpool and at what cost to the peoples of the continent of Africa? Such questions could not legitimately be ignored in Britain's multicultural classrooms, particularly when some pupils were the direct descendants of those whom the British had enslaved. Similarly uncomfortable questions would be asked in respect of the traditional historical treatment of gender and social class.

Thus whereas during the two world wars, consensus history predominated and, in the immediate post-war years, attention turned towards conciliatory history, the 1960s ushered in a period of such fundamental social and educational change that a series of new, and potentially conflicting and competing, histories was bound to emerge. Critics of these new histories could show that some of the new individuals, and groups, were partial, both in their personnel and in their choice of subjects. There were female historians who only wrote about women, Marxist and neo-Marxist historians who only wrote about the working classes. In response, however, it could be cogently argued not only that all historians had to specialize, but also, for example by reference to John Kenyon's *The History Men* (1983), that hitherto history had been written by males, and largely about that political world from which women of all classes and males of the working classes had been almost entirely excluded. Viewed historically, the new emphases were neither essentially conspiratorial, nor revolutionary. Rather, they represented participation and the broadening of democracy, the urgent filling of gaps in what would otherwise remain a partial and one-sided history. They also reflected technological advances. Oral history depended on developments in the use of tape recorders, while the long-established use of primary sources in schools was revolutionized by the advent of commercially-produced 'archive' packs, and by extensive use of the photocopier.

Some of the new historians were to be found in institutions of higher education. There were new universities, as at Sussex, York and Lancaster. The most radical development, the Open University, produced both a new approach to students and a new approach to historical study. Thirty polytechnics were established, and some, for example the Polytechnic of North London and Portsmouth Polytechnic, came to include large and distinguished departments of history. Historical study in such institutions often formed part of a joint degree, so that students and staff became more aware of the particular nature of their discipline in relation to others. There were new historical societies which focused upon particular themes – social history, urban history, oral history, the history of education. Not all the new groups were dominated by professional historians. Some local history societies were led by enthusiasts who had received little formal training in the discipline. The History Workshop Movement, established in 1969 at Ruskin College, Oxford, attempted a more fundamental re-working of the relationship between professional historians and lay people. Local groups, armed with tape recorders and questionnaires, sought to record ordinary voices from the past, and in so doing to reconstruct 'history from below'.

Although during the period of expansion in higher education such groups might operate in a complementary way, when history as a subject of study came under increasing attack, public disputes among historians became more common. Criticism of the Historical Association proceeded both from the polytechnics and from the advocates of reformed school history. Hostility towards the assumption that scholarship was the province of university scholar-gentlemen to be handed down to schools and the general public, and towards universities in general for their exclusion of public-sector historians from the History at the Universities Defence Group, surfaced in the pages of *Past and Present*.[43] In the same journal William Lamont of the University of Sussex took the Historical Association to task for its neglect of the changes which had been taking place in secondary-school history in recent years. Lamont deplored the Historical Association's commitment to 'a discredited tradition of facts-that-must-be-learned chronology', and denied that this tradition could 'be revived without sacrificing our historical integrity'.[44]

Such criticism, however, should not detract from the important role which the Historical Association had played in promoting discussion and development of history teaching both in primary and secondary schools. A new journal, *Teaching History*, was launched in May 1969 and soon won praise from reviewers for 'sticking firmly to its original aim of showing what was going on in the best kind of history lessons', and for seeking 'a remedy for the unpopularity of traditional school history in the age of comprehensive education'.[45] In addition, in 1971 the Association published two influential pamphlets entitled *The Development of Thinking and the Learning of History*, and *Educational Objectives for the Study of History*.[46] In the first of these Jeanette Coltham argued that the selection of topics for study should be based upon the stages in the development of children's thinking outlined by Jean Piaget. In the second, Coltham and John Fines, strongly influenced by the taxonomies of Bloom and Krathwohl and their associates, provided a new emphasis in respect of the purpose of teaching history. For example, a section on 'Skills and Abilities' identified such objectives as 'vocabulary acquisition', 'reference skills', 'memorization', 'comprehension', 'translation', 'analysis', 'extrapolation', 'synthesis', 'judgement and evaluation', and 'communication skills'.[47]

From the 1960s secondary schools were particularly affected by change, with the introduction both of the comprehensive system and of a new examination, the Certificate of Secondary Education. As in the new universities and polytechnics, there were significant opportunities to challenge the nature and style of historical study traditionally associated with the older universities and independent and grammar schools. Some history teachers in secondary schools reorganized their syllabuses around such themes as 'Oppression', or 'Who are the British?'. Others embraced the ethos of the Schools Council History Project which appeared in 1972, with its emphases upon evidence, historical process and historical understanding. Concentration upon historical skills rather than historical facts led inexorably to new methods of assessment. On occasions pupils were judged upon their ability to apply historical skills to previously-unseen historical evidence, and upon their competence in showing empathy with real or imagined historical figures.

Since the Schools Council History Project has excited considerable passions, both for and against, it is particularly important to see this movement in historical perspective. The project was not the product of an extremist fringe, nor simply of teacher-controlled curriculum initiatives, but was based upon what were widely believed to be examples of current good practice. Its topics for study reflected the traditional secondary school history curriculum, and contained a strong British element. Its more contemporary (and controversial) sections, for use with older pupils, were the natural concerns of the early 1970s, for example the Irish question, the Arab-Israeli conflict, the move to European unity, the rise of Communist China.

The project also appeared to be consistent with official thinking. For example, in 1969 Roy Wake, HM Staff Inspector for History, wrote 'that there are no historical facts, only evidence'.[48] David Sylvester, the project's first director, 1972–5, was himself appointed to the inspectorate. Keith Joseph was counted as a supporter, and in 1985 the official stamp of approval was provided by the opening paragraph of *History in the Primary and Secondary Years: An HMI View*, which stated unequivocally that 'History is concerned not with the conveying of accepted facts but with the making of informed judgements, and to the displaying of the evidence on which those judgements are made.'[49] Chapter six on 'Progression and Pedagogy' included a chart of objectives for pupils aged eight to 16 in the following areas: reference and information-finding skills; skills in chronology; language and historical ideas; use and analysis of evidence; empathetic understanding; asking historical questions; synthesis and communication using basic ideas. Chapter seven provided a format for a mark book to assess these seven 'Skills/Concepts/Ideas'.

Thus from the 1960s the one 'best history', if it had ever existed, was replaced, or at least significantly challenged and complemented, by a series of competing histories – for example Marxist history, neo-Marxist history, feminist history, black history, skills-based history. Courses reflecting these new histories became common in the newer institutions of higher education. Changes in agenda and values were accompanied by changes in process and technique. By 1980, 21 of 35 universities and university colleges polled by *The Times Higher Educational Supplement* included a research skills option in their undergraduate courses. By 1988 the figure had risen to 27. Parallel growth over the same period occurred in polytechnics, from six to eight out of 11.[50] Similar changes were also taking place in schools, changes reflected in the GCSE history examinations first taken in 1988.

Kenneth Baker's expression of concern at many of these developments was understandable. His party's, and his own personal identification with 'traditional' historical values is well known, and widely shared. Popular interest in history in this country is not commonly of a revolutionary or questioning nature, but is rather manifested in the heritage approach. This approach encompasses both the great houses of the National Trust, and outdoor museums such as Ironbridge and Beamish which portray, and celebrate, the lives of ordinary people, and is found outside rather than inside the school classroom – in television, films, novels, biographies, and in personal reminiscences.

Conclusion

What conclusions, then, may be drawn about the nature of history in the National Curriculum from the historical perspective? Four points may be made.

The first, and most obvious, is that the place of history in the school curriculum in itself has a history, of which those who are engaged in the contemporary debate should be aware.

Second, perusal of such history shows that, although in theory schools and teachers have had considerable freedom in the twentieth century to construct and control history syllabuses, in fact for many decades there were real, though less visible, control mechanisms at work, and a broad uniformity. From the 1960s, however, changes in society and in education began to produce greater variety. New social groupings, new schools, new examinations, new institutions of higher education, new associations of historians, a new perception of the nature and control of historical knowledge, all played their parts. Such changes, however, did not lead to any marked increase in the popularity of the subject in schools. Though some children, and parents, found the new history more interesting it was still given low ratings for utility. Both the Interim and Final reports of the History Working Group have rightly pointed to the subject's under-representation in many primary schools. Evidence from HMI indicates that history receives little or no attention in two out of three infant classes, and very scant treatment in half of junior schools. Though history is relatively secure in the first three years of secondary schools,'more than half of pupils study no history after the age of 14'.[51] In the light of such evidence the Working Group's conclusion that 'Taken as a whole, school history in England and Wales is varied in quality, quantity and organization' is wholly tenable.[52]

The third point to make is that the Education Reform Act of 1988 can legitimately claim to have begun the process of rescuing school history from its parlous state, and to have made it a foundation subject across the age range of compulsory schooling once more. This, if implemented in full (and signs of retreat are apparent at the time of writing) would represent a most important, indeed a revolutionary, change in the status of the subject within schools. Although some history teachers have been anxious as to the purposes to which a centrally-controlled history curriculum might be put, the list of nine 'purposes of school history', set out on the first page of the Final Report, is an encouraging one which reflects the variety of reasons for which history has been taught in the past.

Finally, it is necessary to draw together the theoretical and historical themes. Though the contemporary arguments among and between historians may be exasperating to politicians, public and pupils alike, they reflect both a long-term debate about the many purposes of the study and teaching of history, and the particular confusions and conflicts of a society which has undergone considerable changes since the 1960s. Even more fundamentally, however, they represent the fact that history in a democracy is the natural product of the contemporary interaction of many groups in society – official, professional and lay – and that the quality of such interaction may be improved by a thorough understanding of its historical antecedents. Any centrally-prescribed school history syllabus which neglects professional experience and wisdom, and which seeks to end the interactive process by which history is constructed, has the capacity to damage not only the quality of history in schools but also the quality of democracy in our society itself.

Notes

1. Cannadine, D. (1987), 'British history: past, present and future'. *Past and Present*, 116, (p. 169).
2. For an example of such analysis see Kliebard, H. (1986), *The Struggle for the American Curriculum, 1893–1958*. London: Routledge.
3. Aldrich, R. (1987), 'Interesting and useful'. *Teaching History*, 47, (pp. 11–14).

4. Joseph, Sir Keith (1984), 'Why teach history in school?' *The Historian*, 2, (p. 10).

5. 'Editorial' (1987), *Teaching History*, 47, (p. 2).

6. Beattie, A. (1987), *History in peril: may parents preserve it*. London: Centre for Policy Studies; Deuchar, S. (1987) *History and GCSE history*. London: Centre for Policy Studies; Kedourie, H. (1988), *Errors and evils of the new history*. London: Centre for Policy Studies; Deuchar, S. (1989), *The new history: a critique*. York: Campaign for Real Education.

7. Department of Education and Science (1987), Press Release 22/87, paragraph 18.

8. For a fuller treatment of the issue of values see Aldrich, R. (1989), 'Class and gender in the study and teaching of history in England in the twentieth century'. *Historical Studies in Education/Revue d'Histoire de l'Education*, 1(1), (pp. 119–135).

9. Quoted in Batho, G. R. (1972), 'Sources for the history of history teaching in elementary schools 1833–1914'. In: T. G. Cook (ed.), *Local Studies and the History of Education*. London: Methuen, (p. 138).

10. Regulations respecting the Education of Pupil Teachers and Stipendiary Monitors, 21st December 1846. In: J. M. Goldstrom (ed.), (1972), *Education. Elementary Education 1780–1900*. Newton Abbot: David and Charles, (pp. 110–118).

11. Batho, op. cit., (p. 139).

12. Ibid. (pp. 139–140).

13. Ibid. (p. 143).

14. Chancellor, V. (1970), *History for their Masters. Opinion in the English History Textbook 1800–1914*. Bath: Adams and Dart, (p. 11).

15. Board of Education (1929), *Handbook of Suggestions for the Consideration of Teachers and others engaged in the Work of Public Elementary Schools*. London: HMSO, (p. 6).

16. Batho, op. cit., (p. 150).

17. Board of Education (1929), *Handbook of Suggestions . . .*, (p. 115).

18. Gordon, P. and Lawton, D. (1978), *Curriculum Change in the Nineteenth and Twentieth Centuries*. London: Hodder and Stoughton, (p. 28); for the nineteenth century see Roach, J. (1976), 'History teaching and examining in secondary schools, 1850–1900'. *History of Education*, 5(2), (pp. 127–40).

19. Board of Education (1908), *Memoranda on Teaching and Organization in Secondary Schools. History*. (Circular 599) London: HMSO, (p. 3).

20. Ministry of Education (1952), *Teaching History*. (Pamphlet 23) London: HMSO, (p. 9).

21. Ibid. (p. 17).

22. Cannadine, D. (1987), op. cit., (p. 176).

23. Incorporated Association of Assistant Masters (1950), *The Teaching of History*. Cambridge: Cambridge University Press, (p. 9).

24. Incorporated Association of Assistant Masters (1965), *The Teaching of History*. Cambridge: Cambridge University Press, (p. 7).
25. Historical Association (1955), *The Historical Association 1906-1956*. London: George Philip, (p. 7).
26. Ibid., (pp. 28, 48).
27. For a fuller account see Aldrich, R. (1984), 'New history: an historical perspective'. In: A. Dickinson, P. Lee and P. Rogers (eds), *Learning History*. London: Heinemann Educational Books (pp. 210–24).
28. Quoted in Chancellor, op. cit., (p. 18).
29. Gilbert, R. (1984), *The Impotent Image. Reflections of Ideology in the Secondary School Curriculum*. Lewes: The Falmer Press, (p. 177).
30. MacInnes, C. M. (1941), *The British Empire and the War*. London: Bell, (pp. 3–4). For an analysis of the imperial theme see Aldrich, R. (1988), 'Imperialism in the study and teaching of history'. In: J. Mangan (ed.), *'Benefits Bestowed'? Education and British Imperialism*. Manchester: Manchester University Press (pp. 23–38).
31. See Elliott, B. J. (1977), 'The League of Nations Union and history teaching in England: a study in benevolent bias'. *History of Education*, 6 (2), (pp. 131–41).
32. League of Nations (1933), *Educational Survey*. Geneva: Secretariat of the League of Nations, (pp. 170–6).
33. See, for example, Lauwerys, J. A. (1953), *History Textbooks and International Understanding*. Paris: Unesco; Dance, E. H. (1954), *History without Bias*. London: Council of Christians and Jews; Hunt, J. W. (ed.) (1954), *English History through Foreign Eyes*. London: George Philip.
34. Reid, R. R., and Toyne, S. M. (1944), *The Planning of a History Syllabus for Schools*. London: King and Staples, (p. 24).
35. Department of Education and Science (1967), *Towards World History*. (Pamphlet 52) London: HMSO, (p. 36).
36. Quoted in Batho, op. cit, (p. 149).
37. Keatinge, M. W. (1910), *Studies in the Teaching of History*. London: Black, (pp. 38–9).
38. Happold, F. C. (1928), *The Approach to History*. London: Christophers, (p. xv).
39. Ibid.
40. Firth, C. B. (1929), *The Learning of History in Elementary Schools*, London: Kegan Paul, Trench, Trubner, (pp. 10–11).
41. Worts, F. R. (1935), *The Teaching of History in Schools. A New Approach*. London: Heinemann, (p. 3).
42. Jeffreys, M. V. C. (1939), *History in Schools: the study of development*. London: Pitman, (pp. 91–4).
43. Coss, P.R. (1988), 'Debate. British history: past, present – and future?'. *Past and Present*, 119, (pp. 171–183).

44. Lamont, W. (1988), 'Debate. British history: past, present – and future?'. *Past and Present*, 119, (p. 193).
45. Coltham, J. B. (1971), *The Development of Thinking and the Learning of History*. London: Historical Association, (p. 44).
46. Coltham, J. B. and Fines, J. (1971), *Educational Objectives for the Study of History*. London: Historical Association.
47. Ibid. (pp. 16–23).
48. Quoted in Burston, W. H. (1972), *Principles of History Teaching*. London: Methuen Educational, (p. 41).
49. Department of Education and Science (1985), *History in the Primary and Secondary Years: An HMI View*. London: HMSO, (p. 1).
50. Richards, H., 'Dating game fades to grey', *The Times Higher Educational Supplement*, 28 April 1989.
51. National Curriculum History Working Group (1990), *Final Report*. London: DES and Welsh Office, (p. 3).
52. National Curriculum History Working Group (1989), *Interim Report*. London: DES and Welsh Office, (pp. 6–8).

Index